Citizens of the
Broken Compass

Ethical and Religious Disorientation
in the Age of Technology

Citizens of the Broken Compass

Ethical and Religious Disorientation in the Age of Technology

Jack E. Brush

BOOKS

Winchester, UK
Washington, USA

First published by iff Books, 2015
iff Books is an imprint of John Hunt Publishing Ltd., Laurel House, Station Approach,
Alresford, Hants, SO24 9JH, UK
office1@jhpbooks.net
www.johnhuntpublishing.com
www.iff-books.com

For distributor details and how to order please visit the 'Ordering' section on our website.

Text copyright: Jack E. Brush 2014

ISBN: 978 1 78279 954 2
Library of Congress Control Number: 2014956732

A CIP catalogue record for this book is available from the British Library.

Design: Stuart Davies

Printed in the USA by Edwards Brothers Malloy

We operate a distinctive and ethical publishing philosophy in all
areas of our business, from our global network of authors to
production and worldwide distribution.

CONTENTS

Preface

The following essays are intended for a thoughtful, but non-technical readership. Very few technical distinctions have been introduced, and the occurrence of foreign languages has been held to a minimum. Furthermore, where a Latin word or phrase does occur, a translation is always provided. The majority of these essays were originally held as talks in several clubs in The Villages in Central Florida, including the Mensa Club, the Freethinkers, Darwinists, Humanists Club and the Civil Discourse Club. I have not attempted to revise significantly the style of the talks, and I have edited them only at points where it was necessary for reading clarity. Chapter 8 "Individual Interests and the Common Good" was conceived from the outset as a written essay and reflects, therefore, a somewhat less personal style. To my colleagues in science, religion and philosophy, my indebtedness to others will be readily apparent. For the general reader, this is, however, of no great consequence, and for this reason I have introduced footnotes only where it seemed absolutely necessary. Finally, I would like to express my appreciation to my wife Susan Brush for her assistance and advice in finalizing this project.

Jack Edmund Brush

Introduction

The "broken compass" strikes me as an appropriate metaphor for a society that ostensibly distinguishes between North and South, East and West—between Just and Unjust, Right and Wrong—but that in truth offers its citizens no reliable orientation in matters of utmost importance. Western society is indeed characterized by ethical and religious disorientation, and we as "Citizens of the Broken Compass" are struggling to find our way, as it were, along a mountain path through a fog of distraction. One is reminded of a line out of Dickens: "The compass is broken, and the exploring party is lost!" The discrepancy alone between our technological achievements and our ethical sensitivities is a glaring reminder of our disorientation. We have developed the technological capability of destroying all life forms on earth either through atomic warfare or through climate change, and yet we have in the same period not developed the ethical sensitivities to make responsible decisions about the available technologies. We are a people today characterized by *technological prowess* and *ethical disorientation*. Since both of these characteristics are rooted in the process of secularization that began already in the seventeenth century, but received its greatest impetus in the so-called Enlightenment period of the eighteenth century, the ethical disorientation cannot be historically or logically separated from the *religious disorientation* which is quite apparent today. The splitting of institutional churches over the role of women or over the rights of the gay/lesbian community cannot be viewed as a strictly ethical difference of opinion; it reflects rather the ethical and religious disorientation that has rendered sound judgment virtually impossible. When one reflects on the history of the Christian Church and recalls that the great controversies were conducted over issues like the doctrine of the Trinity or the efficacy of the Sacrament, one finds it difficult to interpret the events of recent decades as anything other than a reflection of disorientation. This judgment applies not only to Christian groups that are radically conservative, but also to what is left of liberal Christianity. The ethical and religious disorientation is reflected further in the tensions between Christians and Muslims, between "believers" and "non-believers" as well as between theists and atheists. We need to be quite clear about the nature of this disorientation; it is not simply a problem of any particular religious group, but rather a widespread cultural phenomenon. For this reason, I have treated the topics, for the most part, from the standpoint of a critic of contemporary culture. I have attempted to find new possibilities of orientation by discussing the interaction of science and religion, utilizing elements of Stoic philosophy at points (such as natural law and the common good) as well as basic insights of the Judeo-Christian tradition.

In the following essays, I approach the ethical and religious disorientation of Western culture from a number of perspectives, including the problem of self-identity in a secularized world, the debate over same-sex marriage, the question of war and violence, the evolution–creation issue and the fundamentalist under-standing of virgin birth. The essays on the common good and human rights and those on atheism are intended to suggest a path for the future, without making any claim of completeness. Particularly with respect to the issue of same-sex marriage, it seems to me that the ethical and religious disorientation is undeniable. As a nation, the United States is polarized between two views, neither of which can sustain critical examination. Those in favor of same-sex marriage argue from the standpoint of a tolerance that is rooted in the Enlightenment tradition. Those opposing same-sex marriage argue from an ultra-conservative Biblicist standpoint that is rooted in the Puritan tradition. These two traditions, Puritanism and the Enlightenment, have influ-enced American culture from the beginning. According to the first, we need only consult the Bible in order to find the answers to all life's problems; according to the second, we need only apply the principle of tolerance and human rights in order to resolve complex ethical issues. The impasse of these two approaches has rendered serious dialogue impossible and serves as a further indication of the "broken compass" that offers no reliable orientation in the twenty-first century.

The inability of the polarized parties to communicate in any meaningful manner is also apparent in other areas. It is relatively easy, for instance, to support an anti-abortion, pro-war position by referencing selected passages in the Hebrew or in the Christian Bible. It is, however, impossible to carry on a serious discussion with opponents who do not accept the Bible as an absolute ethical rule. It might seem at first glance that the Enlightenment notion of human rights provides a more solid foundation for discussion, but a closer examination reveals that this approach is no less polarizing than the Biblicist approach. In cases of extreme controversy, we are faced with "right" against "right" with no viable way of resolving the issue. In the following essays, I have adopted certain guidelines for constructive dialogue that deviate fundamentally from the Biblicist standpoint and to some extent also from the human rights approach.

1) *There are no absolutes.* That is to say, "black-and-white" answers to ethical or religious questions are not to be attained. Absolute right and absolute wrong are logical abstractions like Isaac Newton's absolute time and absolute space. Such a realization should render us more understanding of the opponent's position; this person might, after all, be right in some respect. Furthermore, all ethical positions are subject to change over time: They are historically conditioned.

2) *All solutions are contextual.* What is ethically acceptable in the society as a whole is not necessarily acceptable within the context of a particular religious community. There is no reason to

expect the entire society to accept the ethical position of a particular religious group. To put it more bluntly, the concept of a "Christian" nation is no more viable in a global world than the concept of an "Islamic" state. It is nothing short of hubris when Christians try to force their values on the entire society. A healthy separation of church and state should allow every citizen to support the nation without being forced to support Christianity or more generally to confess a belief in God. The Pledge of Allegiance and the Apostles' Creed are two historically and materially distinct documents and should not be conflated in the public mind.

3) *The resolution of complex issues requires dialogue employing complementary concepts.* In particular, the concept of human rights must be supplemented by the notion of the common good. Furthermore, justice, understood as a relational concept, is a fundamental category for ethical thinking.

There are historical reasons for the situation in Western society that I describe as the "broken compass", but no attempt has been made in these essays to render an account of the complex processes involved. Perhaps the easiest way to grasp the depth of the problem is to reflect on the polarity between *time* and *eternity*. Underlying the ethical and religious disorientation of our age is the disrupted relationship between time and eternity. Augustine once wrote that he knows perfectly well what "time" is until someone asks him to explain it.[1] Then, he confesses, it becomes very difficult to grasp. Although theologians like Augustine have been deeply concerned about the relationship between time and eternity, the polarity between the two is not exclusively, or even primarily, a religious problem. Rather, it is fundamentally a philosophical problem that has challenged thinkers from Plato and Aristotle down to Martin Heidegger and Alfred North Whitehead.

Let us begin with an everyday situation. If you ask someone the question: "What time is it?", you will undoubtedly receive an answer involving numbers, for instance: "It is 12:30 p.m." Such an answer is so common in our everyday lives that we rarely reflect upon the connection between *time* and *numbers*. Every household has at least one clock; public buildings have clocks; many town squares have clocks; and many individuals wear a wrist watch daily. All of these devices are provided with numbers so that we can determine the correct time. If we have only two hours to perform a certain task, we need to know how much time has elapsed since we began. From this, we can draw a further conclusion. Time not only has something to do with *numbers*, time is *measurable*. Then measuring is one of the primary functions of numbers. If we adopt our "clock-time" as fundamental, we arrive at a linear view of time as a series of points, each of which follows the one before it and all of which can be counted. Applying this view of time to the life of a human being, life seems to be a one-way street which leads from birth to death, with no possibility of turning back and with no possibility of continuing indefinitely.

In this context, eternity is often considered to be the state of the individual *after* death, and for this reason, eternity is thought to be synonymous with *afterlife*. This usage of the word "eternity" is, however, unsatisfactory because it indicates a further point in the series. It is as if the life of the person took place in time from point A to point B, and then afterlife began at point C and continued forever. But afterlife in this sense is *everlasting*, not *eternal*. The word "eternity" has in the philosophical as well as in the theological tradition a different meaning, and this meaning can only be grasped if we move beyond the "clock-time" which is so predominant in our society.

Trying to think about time without numbers will strike us at first as an odd endeavor because the linear view of time as a series of points was the basis of classical physics in the seventeenth and eighteenth centuries and is still primary today in the natural sciences. Nevertheless, the grammatical structure of the

English language points us immediately in a different direction by distinguishing three modes of time: past, present and future. Events that have already occurred belong to the past; events that are taking place now belong to the present; and events that have not yet occurred belong to the future. It is interesting to note that we can discuss these modes of time without reference to numbers. Still, it may seem at first glance that the modes of time represent a series like our clock-time, albeit a series that begins with past and ends with future. The apparent similarity with clock-time is, however, only an illusion, and as soon as we introduce the other tenses, namely present perfect, past perfect and future perfect, we realize that the modes of time describe events and their relevance, not points in a series. Both the past tense and the present perfect tense refer to a completed event, but they refer to it differently. The present perfect tense indicates relevance for the present that is not expressed in the past tense. "I have lived here for three years" does not have the same meaning as "I lived here for three years." Or consider the present tense. "He eats cereal for breakfast" does not mean that he did this at *one* point in a series, but rather that he does it habitually, i.e. at *many* points in time. The attempt to correlate the modes of time with points in a series is frustrated at every turn for the following reason. *Time as a series of points has an essential connection with numbers, whereas time as a description of events is inherently related to language.* Just as the words in a sentence hang together and convey a meaning, the modes of time are interrelated and enable unified experiences. The interrelatedness of past, present and future is apparent in the experience of promise and fulfillment; what was promised in the past and anticipated in the future is fulfilled in the present. Past, present and future are not three *points* in a series, but a *unified experience*, which brings us to a new understanding of eternity. Plato once described time as the "moving image of eternity", whereby he meant that time and eternity were not to be separated as though eternity were timeless.[2] Time and eternity belong together, and in some way, time reflects eternity: It is the moving image of eternity. For our purposes, it suffices to say that eternity is the perfection or completion of time so that time occurs in its purity as an integrated whole. In the experience of eternity *in* time, everything has its place, nothing is lost.

In our technological age, this experience of eternity in time has been obscured by the predominance of clock-time. Should the bond between time and eternity ever be totally severed, we would cease to be human beings, but the situation today is so extreme that we can appropriately say that eternity is no longer a part of our conscious experience. What we experience day after day is time as a series of points and our lives as a one-way street. Without the unifying of time by eternity, we struggle to hold time together. We try to stabilize the self through the consumption of goods. We seek religious views that are absolute, and we apply ethical standards that are no longer grounded in our own experience of time and eternity.

1

Consumerism and the Problem of Self-Identity

The blurring of the boundary between cultural experience and consumerism is one of the dominant elements of modern Western societies. If you enjoy visiting museums, pay careful attention to the experience at your next opportunity. In almost every major museum, you will find yourself at some point—usually at the end of your visit—in the gift shop where you are encouraged to participate not in a cultural experience, but rather in consumerism. "Please buy something before you leave!" is the message. So what was this experience of visiting a museum? Was it about art appreciation or about the economy? Was it about understanding and appreciating distant cultures and distant times or was it about being a consumer? What was the point of buying a cheap little replica of the Parthenon in the Acropolis Museum after you had marveled at the classic balance of the real thing?

Consumerism in its modern form is an integral part of a larger process of the economization of society. By "economization", I do not mean the "economizing", which would be at least an environmentally sound venture, but rather the converting of all values into economic terms. The economization of society means that all decisions are ultimately made on the basis of economic calculations. Whether we are talking about purchasing a new house, hiring a professor at a university, or getting married, all decisions are determined by an economic analysis. Internationally recognized in this area of research is Gary Becker, an economist who studied under Milton Friedman at the University of Chicago and who won the Nobel Prize in Economics in 1992 for his extension of economic theory to human behavior.[3] Today, I cannot discuss this process further, but I mention it because consumerism is a part of this larger process.

Focusing our attention now on consumerism itself, we think immediately of the fast-food industry, of internet companies like Amazon, of the day-after-Thanksgiving Christmas sales and so forth. So dominant is consumerism in American society that even Europeans often think that it began in the United States. When you consider that there is, for instance, a McDonald's in 190 countries, the notion that consumerism is an American invention seems obvious. In this case, however, the obvious is not correct. In contrast to the generally accepted opinion, consumerism as a modern phenomenon began in Europe and only later spread to the US. It is helpful, I think, to distinguish several phases of consumerism in order to see clearly the role that self-identity plays.

Modern consumerism began to develop in Western Europe around the middle of the eighteenth century. In its second phase, it spread to the United States, and thereafter the US became the primary force in further developing consumerism in the twentieth century. Today, consumerism is a global phenomenon of enormous proportions.[4] Since I have already mentioned McDonald's, let's stay with the culinary example for a moment and see how consumerism began. We take it for granted that there are restaurants in every city, in every small community and on almost every street corner where we can enjoy a meal. There are fast-food restaurants, and there are very exclusive restaurants, but no matter where you are, there are restaurants. However, it was not always so. If we go back to the Middle Ages or even to the Renaissance, we won't find any restaurants. To be sure, there were guest houses where travelers could have a meal and spend the night before continuing their journey. But restaurants in the modern sense didn't exist—localities where people went to enjoy dining out as a form of entertainment. The first restaurants of this sort sprang up in eighteenth-century Europe for reasons that are not totally clear. At the same time, the experience of consumerism spread to other areas of life where new products became available. Coffee and tea became available in Europe. Cotton was imported at first from India and then produced in Europe itself. The middle class was emerging, and there was new prosperity that made the consumption of new products possible. And yet, neither the availability of new products nor the prosperity of the new middle class explains sufficiently the revolutionary attitude of consumerism.

The old European aristocracy of the seventeenth century exhibited notably less interest in consumable goods than the new middle class of the eighteenth century. The members of the aristocracy tended to be more traditional in their values and customs; their thinking focused more on preserving what they already owned than on acquiring something new. Furthermore, they tended to be constrained to some extent by traditional ethical and moral values about temperance and moderation—values rooted in religious convictions. Before consumerism could really blossom, traditional religious values had to be swept away, and that is precisely what happened during the European Enlightenment of the eighteenth century. The "Age of Reason", as it was proclaimed, was the first cultural revolution in European history that was not oriented toward the past. The Renaissance was, in contrast, a rediscovering of the Greek and Roman classics. But the "Age of Reason" was different. It didn't value the past for what it could offer the present; instead, it brought about a radical break with the past so that new values guided by reason alone could prevail. Viewed from the stand-point of reason, there seems to be no convincing objection to consuming new products and goods at will. There is no logical reason against enjoying a new cotton garment from India, no reason not to enjoy dining out, no *reason* at all! With this shift in thinking, a Pandora's Box was opened that has led to a practical hedonism in Western societies, the last consequences of which we have not yet seen. The entire entertainment industry is based on hedonist thinking and thrives on the insatiable desire for pleasure that today has become globalized.

Before proceeding further, the events of the eighteenth century require our attention a bit longer. We have already mentioned the increased availability of products and goods, the new prosperity of the middle class, the erosion of religious values and the emergence of a nascent hedonism, but there was an additional factor in the eighteenth century that drove consumerism, and it is precisely this element that has become paramount today. The Europeans of the eighteenth century experienced an *identity crisis* of the first order. The breakdown of the aristocratic structure, the erosion of traditional values and particularly the emergence of the middle class disrupted all levels and segments of society. Suddenly, former plebeians became merchants, and the common people had money to buy the new products. As the merchants became more and more prosperous, the social position of the aristocracy became more and more dubious. As the aristocratic titles of birth such as Sir, Lady, Lord, Duke, Duchess and Squire became more and more irrelevant, the earned academic titles became more and more important. If you didn't have the inherited title "Duke", you might be able with sufficient effort to earn the title "Doctor".

Parallel to this change in the use of titles, consumerism became the hallmark of success and served to establish the identity of the individual in society. Determinative for an individual's social status was no longer his family, but rather his financial ability to consume. Well, to be more accurate: It wasn't a matter of *ability* to consume, but rather the *actual* consumption. The ability had to be manifested in order to function effectively in establishing identity. In a small village where everyone knows everyone else, and everyone knows everyone else's financial situation, the actual manifestation of wealth may be less important, but in the second half of the eighteenth century, the population in Europe increased dramatically so that the small village atmosphere was often replaced by a more cosmopolitan setting characterized by a certain anonymity. In England, for instance, the population doubled between 1750 and 1800. In dealing with strangers, ability counts for little if that ability is not manifested. In short, actual consumption became a major avenue for establishing personal identity and securing a position in society.

By 1850, consumerism had finally reached America, and in Europe, it entered a new phase: *leisure time* consumption. The first soccer club was founded in England in 1858, and around the same time, travel bureaus like Thomas Cook were established. Dancing became very popular as a leisure-time activity, and by 1860, there were 68 dance halls in Paris. Meanwhile in the US, the American engineer George Ferris Jr developed the Ferris Wheel for the Chicago Exposition in 1893, and his invention soon became a popular source of amusement on both sides of the Atlantic. Even more important, however, was the development of the film industry. By 1900, American and European movies had become very popular, and by 1918, Universal Studios had international branches in countries like Indonesia, Japan and India. The consumer possibilities offered by amusement centers and by the film industry replaced step by step the traditional forms of leisure-time activity in the home such as reading a book aloud to family and friends, playing musical instruments, singing songs and engaging in stimulating conversation.

After the Second World War, consumerism entered a third phase. Just as the shop was the symbol of the first phase and the department store the symbol of the second, the shopping mall became the symbol of the third. The shopping mall combines several forms of consumption under one roof: the purchase of products and goods, the experience of dining in a fast-food or in a more elegant restaurant, the amusement of games, etc. If we look at consumerism in the last quarter of the twentieth century, there are several characteristics that stand out clearly. Most noticeably, consumerism has become global—certainly global in the sense that you can purchase almost the same products anywhere in the developed world, but also global in the sense that consumer preferences have become uniform worldwide. Whether in New York, Tokyo or Zurich, people desire more or less the same products of consumption. Peter Stearns has termed this phenomenon: "the global transformation of desire".[4]

We leave now the history of consumerism and turn our attention to two developments in the last quarter of the twentieth century that have had significant impact on the relation between consumerism and identity building. One of these developments was political-economic; the other was philosophical. The economic consequences of the 1973 oil crisis, the increasing international competition coming from countries such as China, and the decline in the real income of many American families led to a decline in the aggregate demand for goods and services. All political and economic indicators pointed to a decline in consumption at a time when consumption had become the driving force of capitalism. During the ensuring decades, American business at all levels was faced with the problem of motivating Americans to consume, even if the consumer was not financially in a position to do so. Since my topic is not economics, I am omitting here all details; the economic development from 1973 to the housing crisis of 2008 is an extremely complicated matter and still a topic of dispute. Nevertheless, one thing is sufficiently clear. The solution to the problem of motivating the consumer was consumer credit. Whether it was easy access to credit cards or low mortgage rates for home buyers, all possible steps were taken to encourage consumption.

Prior to these political-economic events, a new philosophy had been developing known as postmodernism, and central to postmodernism was a radical view of self-identity. To put it in the simplest terms, postmodern philosophy rejected the notion of innate qualities in the soul or the mind of the individual and claimed that self-identity is nothing more than a social construct. The individual is not born with any tendencies toward a particular self-concept, be it sexual or otherwise, and therefore the individual is totally free to construct an identity for himself. (One of the chief proponents of this view was the French philosopher Michel Foucault.) Furthermore, there is no right or wrong way to build self-identity. There are no criteria for saying that this self-identity is authentic and that one is not: All possible understandings of self-identity are equally valid.

These philosophical ideas were a boon for consumer research theorists who quickly adopted them and developed theories about the so-called postmodern consumer. In a 2003 article in the *Journal of Industrial Psychology*, the authors compare the modern with the postmodern consumer:

> Turning to (the) consumer, it is observable that the modern consumer valued the functionality and utility value of a specific product or service, and the ability of this product or service to solve his/her "problem", while the postmodern consumer is less concerned with this. He/she is focused on a more intangible "problem", that of building a *sense of self* or *identity* in a highly dynamic, complex and fragmented society, and is consequently more interested in the symbolic or cultural value that a specific product or service projects.[5(p5)]

Whereas the earlier consumer theories tended to view production as positive and excessive consumption as negative, the postmodern consumer theories celebrate the value of consumption for establishing personal identity and stability of the self. The self-identity of the modern consumer was rooted in the individual's occupation, religious affiliation and social status. This individual sought to maintain or even increase his social status and was prone to purchase objects of relative permanence as symbols of social status, whether that status had already been acquired or was merely desired. In contrast, the self-identity of the postmodern consumer is created through consumption and requires constant developing and reaffirming. This individual is less likely to be attracted to objects of permanence and at the same time very prone to seek out consumable objects that have the necessary symbolic value for identity building. This doesn't mean, of course, that postmodern consumers *never* purchase objects of permanence, but when they do, these objects soon lose for them their value for identity building. That is, their value is consumed. The modern consumer may *abuse* a work of art for selfish motives; he may view it only in terms of its monetary exchange value and its function as a status symbol. But the postmodern consumer literally *consumes* its value; this person devours the work of art in the process of identity building and leaves the physical object as an empty shell. The work of art has lasting value for the modern consumer, but only transitory for the postmodern consumer. This individual must move on quickly to some other object in a never-ending attempt to establish identity and stabilize the self through consumption. For this reason, the postmodern consumer tends to seek entertainment, not culture, and the film industry has been ready at hand to transform any and all aspects of culture into the form of affordable entertainment. Not even the religious texts of the Judeo-Christian tradition have escaped the hands of the entertainment makers in Hollywood. In the case of films, the identity building occurs first of all through the selection of films to be consumed, then through identification with certain actors and actresses.

As we have already seen, the identity-establishing function of consumption was an important element in eighteenth-century Europe. But in the last quarter of the twentieth century, this process acquired unprecedented proportions through the unqualified endorsement of corporate America. Supported by philosophical analysis and easily propagated by an ever-expanding advertising industry, the notion of identity building through consumption served well the needs of corporate leaders. If you want "ruggedness" to be a part of your self-identity, identify with the guy on the horse and smoke Marlboro. Smoking Marlboro is objective. Everyone can see it. Your position in society is established and your sense of self, your self-identity, is affirmed. There is, of course, the problem that you might eventually end up in a hospital bed instead of on the horse, that your sense of ruggedness might wane with the chronic cough, but the less secure we are in ourselves and the more difficulty we have in establishing a sense of self or self-identity, the more susceptible we are to the postmodern claim of finding ourselves through consumption. For those of you who know the history of advertising, I add as a footnote: The concept of the Marlboro man was developed already in 1954, but the famous advertising campaign with Wayne McLaren began in 1976. McLaren died in 1992 at the age of 51 with lung cancer.

These reflections on self-identity and consumerism have relevance for our entire society and could be discussed from the standpoint of their political or environmental significance. Today, however, I will only mention their relevance for the Baby-boomers who are now beginning to move into retirement. I used to organize an annual seminar for new retirees of Mercedes Benz in Switzerland because the company recognized the identity crisis that many retirees experience. It seems to me that the problem is exacerbated in retirement communities in the States because of the discontinuity in personal relationships. Here we have a community of individuals who have no previous experience in communicating with each other. A retirement community is a collection of individuals from quite diverse backgrounds: social, financial, educational and political. It is true that the mass media has provided some degree of uniformity, but it is equally true that nobody really knows who's who in these communities—a fact that intensifies the identity crisis.

I had an uncle of whom I was very fond. He joined the US Navy the day after Pearl Harbor, and following the war, he became a career Navy man. Yet after he retired, he was never seen wearing any garment bearing the word "Navy": no Navy sweatshirt, no Navy bill cap, nothing. In contrast, garments with military insignia abound in retirement communities of the Babyboomers. In Florida, you can't go shopping in the local supermarket without seeing military bill caps. Why is that? I suggest to you that it has to do with self-identity. In a community where you are unknown, you can establish your identity by purchasing and wearing regularly a military cap. Or consider the cars that we buy. Does one buy a moderately priced vehicle for transportation or a specialty item to bolster a sense of self? Is the primary consideration utility or self-identity? There is, of course, nothing wrong with buying a specialty item, but one should be aware from the outset that self-identity cannot really be established through the consumption of tangible objects. You may become possessed by your possessions, but you won't attain a stable sense of self. So the problem of self-identity remains. Who am I? Do others see me as I really am? Or do I even know who I really am? What is it in my core that provides continuity in time and space? What is it that allows me a unified experience of the diverse world around me? Who am I really? That's the problem of self-identity.

If we ask the deeper question about the causes for the identity crisis of Western societies, we will find the answer, at least in part, in the severing of time from eternity. It was in previous historical periods the experience of eternity *in* time that gave a sense of stability to the self and that allowed the formation of an enduring self-identity. Whether this insight is viewed from the standpoint of a religious tradition or in a purely philosophical manner, the fundamental point remains the same: It is the reflection of eternity in time that unifies the manifold of experience and allows the self to establish its identity. Thrown into the flux of time without any point of orientation, having lost the sense of eternity in time, the self struggles to stabilize itself through various means. One of these has been through consumption. This may be a gift for corporations, but it's a disaster for the individual.

2

The Case for and against Same-Sex Marriage

One of the leading proponents of same-sex marriage wrote in an article appearing in May 2014: "The movement for same-sex marriage has been politically triumphant, but its case is incomplete because the arguments against it have not been understood."[6(p431)] The author of this statement is himself not gay; Andrew Koppelman is married, has three children and is engaged as professor of law and political science at Northwestern University School of Law. In his opening statement, Koppelman makes two claims with which I concur completely. Firstly, same-sex marriage has been politically triumphant, but, secondly, it has been triumphant for the wrong reasons. Whether we attribute the growing public acceptance of same-sex marriage to the numbing effect of Hollywood, which decided some time ago to support the gay/lesbian movement, or whether it is the reluctance of the public to engage seriously in ethical and political discussion, or whether it reflects the nihilistic tendencies of our age, the simple fact remains: The crucial issues involved in the acceptance or rejection of same-sex marriage have not been seriously discussed by the American public. I find this state of affairs unworthy of a democratic society.

When we consider that the institution of marriage in its traditional form has a history in Western civilization of at least 2500 years, a movement to change this fundamental institution deserves more than Hollywood movies and cheap political slogans. Perhaps Socrates was wrong when he restricted homosexuality in the *Symposium* to non-physical relationships. Perhaps the views of Plato, Aristotle and Cicero were wrong.

Perhaps Augustine, Thomas Aquinas and many other thinkers were wrong. Perhaps in our technological wisdom, we understand the world better than they did, but to overthrow 2500 years of tradition requires in my opinion serious thought and discussion not only among politicians, but also among attorneys of law, philosophers of ethics and above all among the citizens of our democracy. So the purpose of my talk is not to convince you of an argument for or against same-sex marriage, but rather to motivate you to serious reflection and discussion.

Before we consider some of the arguments, we need to draw several distinctions that are often overlooked. The whole question of same-sex marriage can be considered from various points of view. We could consider it within the context of a particular religion—say, for instance, Christianity or Judaism. Or we could consider it as a moral or ethical question that concerns our society as a whole. Finally, we could consider it from a legal standpoint and present arguments for the enactment of new laws. It seems to me that it should be possible for reasonable persons to agree that religious considerations are appropriate only, or at least primarily, in the context of the religion in question. A Christian might decide, for example, that same-sex marriage is inconsistent with Christian faith and, therefore, unacceptable in the context of this religion. The same person could decide, however, that at this particular point in history, given the structure of our society, same-sex marriage is sensible and ethically defensible. Trying to separate neatly the ethical and the political issues is in my opinion more difficult. We could take the position that the government should not regulate by law any matters of ethics, but that is a difficult position to defend consistently. We consider murder to be not only illegal, but also immoral. We think of incest as immoral, not just illegal. So the boundary between the two is somewhat fluid. Nevertheless, for the purpose of discussion, we can bracket out initially the legal issues and raise the question about the morality of same-sex marriage, realizing that in a second stage we may want to incorporate some of our conclusions into law.

So what is the moral case for same-sex marriage? If we set aside the legal arguments about constitutional rights, antidiscrimination laws and the like and focus on the moral issue, the argument usually goes something like this: Opponents of same-sex marriage describe in detail the moral value of heterosexual marriage. But same-sex marriage is not fundamentally different from heterosexual marriage. Therefore, same-sex marriage enjoys the same moral status as heterosexual marriage. It is interesting to note that the moral case for same-sex marriage takes as its starting point the moral worth of heterosexual marriage. To date, I have found no moral argument for same-sex marriage that is independent of the traditional concept of marriage. So let's take a closer look at the moral worth of traditional heterosexual marriage. I will simplify the matter by limiting my comments to the writings of John Finnis, Professor of Law and Legal Philosophy at Oxford University and Professor of Law at the University of Notre Dame.

John Finnis belongs to a group of Roman Catholic scholars who oppose same-sex marriage on the basis of the concept of natural law.[7] Natural law (*lex naturalis*) was originally a Stoic idea, which was taken over by Cicero, then later by Augustine and Thomas Aquinas. As Finnis understands marriage, it has moral worth on two levels; the first is personal, the second is societal. On a personal level, marriage is morally good because it is based on mutual trust and commitment. Marriage involves the willingness and commitment to belong to one's spouse and to be united with this person in body and mind. It is a unique form of communion and friendship. The moral worth of marriage has also a societal dimension because it involves the procreation, nurture and education of children who will themselves be moving out into society. Finnis emphasizes repeatedly that each human being has one mother and one father, and that the mother and father are not only necessary for the procreation of the child, but that they are also uniquely suited to nurture and educate the child. As Finnis understands it, marriage belongs to natural law because it is reasonable; that is, there are good reasons for the institution of marriage. It is ultimately necessary for the continuing stability of society. Finnis is opposed to same-sex marriage because he doesn't think that any such claim can be made for it.

The proponents of same-sex marriage respond to this by saying that the same moral worth could be realized between partners of the same sex. Between two men or between two women, the same type of commitment could be made. Same-sex marriage also involves the willingness and commitment to belong to one's partner and to be united with this person in body and mind. It is also a unique form of communion and friendship. And as far as the societal dimension is concerned, same-sex couples could adopt children and provide the same nurture and education as heterosexual couples. Viewed properly, the marriage relationship between two persons of the same sex is not fundamentally different from the marriage relationship of the infertile heterosexual couple that might decide to adopt children. Given that there are children who need a good home, the acceptance of same-sex marriage could be a great benefit to society.

John Finnis has responded to this argument by claiming that it is artificial. In his mind, the gay and lesbian community has adopted the moral case for traditional marriage and artificially substituted a same-sex partner into it. Taking a simple analogy, we could summarize his argument in this way: It is as though one replaced the battery in a flashlight with a new one that had two positive or two negative poles instead of a positive and a negative. Who seriously thinks that the flashlight will provide the same light as before? To be precise, Finnis maintains that the element of procreation is always at work in the marriage relationship; it is the awareness of being involved in this life-process that makes the relationship so unique. Even the infertile couple is involved in this life-process, and such a claim cannot be made for the same-sex couple. The only possible motivation for intimate same-sex relationships is, according to Finnis, pleasure because close relationships and friendships between persons of the same sex do not require sexual intercourse. So unless we want to abandon moral arguments altogether and resign ourselves to a crass form of hedonism, we should oppose same-sex marriage. At first reading, Finnis' argument may seem convincing, but his restriction of sexual relationships to intercourse of the procreative kind has consequences for heterosexual marriage as well. In order to preserve consistency, he must reject any sexual activity within a heterosexual marriage that deviates from the established norm. For example, fellatio within a heterosexual marriage cannot qualify as sexual intercourse of a procreative kind any more than it could within a homosexual marriage. In view of this, it is difficult to imagine how Finnis' position could gain wide acceptance outside of strict Roman Catholic circles.

At this point, we seem to be at an impasse. Andrew Koppelman summarizes the situation well:

> The controversy over same-sex marriage…is a battle between two moral visions. According to one, sex can be morally worthy precisely and only because of its place in procreation. Even the marriages of infertile heterosexual couples take their meaning from the fact that they form a union of the procreative kind, and their bodily union therefore has procreative significance…According to the other moral vision, sex is valuable because it draws us toward friendship of a singular degree and kind. This bringing together of persons has intrinsic worth, whether or not it leads to childbearing or childrearing.[8(p1646)]

In order to resolve the controversy, Koppelman suggests that we apply the analogy of religious tolerance. After the Protestant Reformation of the sixteenth century, there were wars fought in Europe between Catholics and Protestants, each side claiming to be the authentic form of Christianity. As we know from history, the resolution was not to be found in the adjudication of the conflicting claims, but rather in the notion of religious tolerance. Today, we have come to think of religion as a very broad category, which includes not only Roman Catholicism and the Protestant denominations, but also Judaism, Buddhism, Hinduism and Islam, and toward those whose religious views we do not share, we adopt a moral attitude of tolerance. According to Koppelman, a similar attitude of tolerance would resolve the issue of same-sex marriage. This is indeed a very intriguing proposal, but there are problems with the analogy. In the case of religious tolerance of the Enlightenment period, the citizenry was faced, for the most part, with established institutions, which it wanted to treat equally. In contrast, heterosexual and homosexual marriages are not two well-established institutions, which we could view with tolerance. The inclusion of same-sex marriage, i.e. the expansion of the definition of marriage to include same-sex couples, would in effect create a new institution. The new definition of marriage would have to be more abstract than the traditional one; marriage would no longer be understood as a relationship between a man and a woman, but rather between two persons. That might be an appropriate move, but it needs to be discussed.

In the literature for and against same-sex marriage, we are confronted repeatedly with the problem of definition. If we define marriage broadly enough, there seems to be no reasonable argument for excluding same-sex couples. Understood as an intimate relationship between two persons, which involves sexual intercourse, a strong commitment to each other and the mutual sharing of resources, there seems to be no reason to exclude those cases where the two persons are of the same sex. If, on the other hand, we add to the above definition the further clause that marriage involves the active participation in a characteristically human life-process, same-sex couples would be excluded because their sexual relationship can in no way be interpreted as participation in this life-process. On the contrary, same-sex couples are dependent on the life-process of heterosexual couples for their very existence. Why then should society view homosexual relationships as equal in value to heterosexual ones? Of course, we could respond by pointing out that human relationships are primarily existential in character and that the life-process of nature is not relevant in this realm. Regardless of how the two persons are generated, whether as the outcome of a natural life-process or as the result of technological cloning in the laboratory, the two persons are here and now existentially capable of building a marriage relationship equal to that of a heterosexual couple. This answer seems to require, however, a separation of human existence from natural processes and illustrates well some of the underlying philosophical concerns involved in defining marriage.

The ancient Greek philosopher Heraclitus wrote around 500 BC: "All things come into being through opposition…" Nature seems to like contrasts and oppositions: positive and negative electric charges, electric fields and magnetic fields creating what we call light, north and south poles, up and down spin of electrons, etc. Likewise, the natural life-process in higher animals requires a contrast of sexes. But maybe all of this has no relevance to marriage. Perhaps we should abstract from all of this in order to define marriage, just as the mathematician abstracts from the concrete reality around him in order to define a right triangle or a straight line. Or perhaps the oppositions of nature are precisely the essential elements to be considered in defining marriage. This is one of the decisions that needs to be made in discussing same-sex marriage—not a decision to be made by Hollywood, by the news media, or by religious leaders speaking from a particular religious perspective. It is a decision to be made by us as responsible citizens of a democracy.

So far, we have been considering the case for and against same-sex marriage as presented by two authors, Andrew Koppelman and John Finnis, neither of whom belong to the gay/lesbian community. There is, however, one set of arguments from the gay/lesbian community that must be mentioned, namely, the arguments *against* same-sex marriage. It is not a universally accepted or even a majority opinion in the gay/lesbian community that same-sex marriage would be a step forward. Many of those in this community hold the view that marriage in any form is a constraining, oppressive institution in which gays and lesbians should not participate. They maintain that sexual pleasure is a good in itself that need not be connected to any long-term relationship in order to be morally valuable. Paula Ettelbrick, an attorney who was one of the pioneers of the gay, lesbian, bisexual and transsexual movement in the United States, published an article in 1989 entitled "Since When Is Marriage a Path to Liberation?", in which she questioned the appropriateness of same-sex marriage as a goal for the gay/lesbian community.[9] In 2004, she along with Julie Shapiro published another article—a conversation between the two of them—entitled "Same-Sex Marriage: Are We on the Path to Liberation Now?", in which she admitted: "Lately I've been getting a little scared because people have proposed that we should move away from the 'gay pride image'—meaning a display of the full diversity of our community—and just promote the 'same-sex marriage image' to advance the movement."[10(p490)]

To be sure, Ettelbrick's views do not represent the entire gay/lesbian community; nevertheless, her sentiments are by far not an isolated case among gays and lesbians. *The Nation* magazine published an article by Gabriel Rotello in 1997, which concludes with these words:

The antimarriage sentiment in the gay and lesbian political world has abated in recent years, and the legalization of same-sex marriage is now an accepted focus of gay liberation. Yet prevention activists generally don't include marriage as a goal because they generally don't include monogamy as a goal...Meanwhile, most advocates of same-sex marriage fail to make the case for AIDS prevention because they are generally careful not to make the case for marriage, but simply for the *right* to marriage. This is undoubtedly good politics, since many if not most of the major gay and lesbian organizations that have signed on to the fight for same-sex marriage would instantly sign off at any suggestion that they were actually encouraging gay men and lesbians to marry.[11(p16)]

For many in the gay/lesbian community, the push for same-sex marriage appears to be a political battle about the rights of gays and lesbians and seems to have less to do with any moral stance about marriage. These voices offer no moral case for same-sex marriage, but rather a moral case for diversity, i.e. a case for same-sex relationships as such. It is worth remembering that the gay/lesbian movement started in 1969 with the Stonewall Riots in Greenwich Village, New York, and as the literature clearly indicates, the movement still bears some of the marks of this radical phase, such as a deep distrust of traditional institutions and a desire to develop an alternative lifestyle. The gay/lesbian community is a part of the legacy of the 1960s, and it may well be in the interest of this community as well as of the entire society to respect it as such; the alternative lifestyle of the gay/lesbian community remains a testimony to how much was achieved and how much still remains to be done.

Without question, the disagreements within the gay/lesbian community on the issue of same-sex marriage complicate the matter for society as a whole. Nevertheless, society as a whole should come to some resolution, based on serious thought and open dialogue, about the status of same-sex marriage in the twenty-first century, even if the gay/lesbian community is not unified on the issue. As citizens in a democratic society, we bear this responsibility.

3

From Murder to War

The prohibition against murder is a fundamental law of organized society. As soon as human beings organized themselves into social units, it became necessary to restrict their behavior in certain ways, and one of the basic ways of providing the stability of the group was to forbid taking the life of a fellow member. This statement seems to hold true whether we are considering very primitive societies or highly developed technological societies. Murder is the ultimate disruption of the social unit, and from this standpoint, the prohibition against murder was, practically speaking, a necessary condition for the promulgation of the group. The prohibition against murder had, however, a further dimension. If only vaguely, the members of the group sensed that there was something sacred about life, and therefore the taking of the life of another human being was understood as an offense against the gods. With time, it was also recognized that murder was an offense against humanity itself. Human life is a shared experience, and to kill another human being is to destroy something within the perpetrator himself. In the seventeenth century, the Englishman John Donne brought this thought to expression in his famous *Meditation* XVII, a line of which served later as the title for one of Hemingway's novels:

No man is an island, entire of itself; every man is a piece of the continent, a part of the main. If a clod be washed away by the sea, Europe is the less, as well as if a promontory were, as well as if a manor of thy friend's or of thine own were: any man's death diminishes me, because I am involved in mankind, and therefore never send to know for whom the bell tolls; it tolls for thee.

Given the outward prohibition against murder and the inward aversion to murder, it is not at all clear how to make the leap from rejecting murder to accepting war. If the taking of *one* human life is considered abominable, why is the taking of hundreds of *thousands* of human lives considered acceptable? That this question has troubled humanity for millennia is evidenced by the fact that various models for understanding war have been developed. Today, I will focus on three models that seem to me historically significant and currently relevant. These models do not claim to be exhaustive nor do they necessarily occur in pure form. Bear in mind that they overlap at points and that there are gradations between them. Nevertheless, these models serve to orientate our thinking about the problem of war, and they can, I believe, be easily applied to our world. I call these three models: the *Holy War*, the *Just War* and the *Honorable War*. All three models have this in common: They serve to separate the killing that occurs in war from the prohibition against murder so that war appears not only to be acceptable, but in some strange sense to be an irrefutably worthy endeavor.

The Holy War

All three of the well-known monotheistic religions, Judaism, Christianity and Islam, have practiced at one time or another holy war. It is not clear that monotheism is a necessary condition for the concept of holy war, but it does seem to imbue the notion with a sense of the unconditional. The thinking seems to have proceeded along these lines. Since there is only one God and this God commands us to wage war, there can be no mitigating circumstances, no deferments, no exceptions. Irrational as it may seem, the God who issued the command against murder commands in this particular case mass murder. Although the phrase "holy war" was first coined at the beginning of the nineteenth century, the concept itself is quite old and has its roots in the religious mentalities of the Ancient Near East. In the following, I will concentrate on the early Hebrew and Jewish tradition because the sources are readily available. The same case could be made in the context of Christianity or Islam. As I have said, all three monotheistic religions have practiced holy war. Within Christianity, it was termed "Crusades"; within Islam, it is called a "Jihad".

If we look at the history of Israel from its Hebrew origins through the conquest of Canaan, the development of a monarchy, the exiles, the Maccabean Revolt, the Great Revolt which resulted in the destruction of the second Temple, down to the aftermath of the Bar Kokhba Rebellion in the second century AD, we find that the notion of a holy war developed very early and reached its greatest influence during the period of the Judges. In that period, the tribes of Israel were held together in a loose confederacy for the common worship of Yahweh and for common military action. Since holy war is a *religious* idea, it presupposes a military understanding of God. We find this clearly reflected in the Song of Moses (Exodus 15.3), where we read: "Yahweh is a man of war." The holy war is commanded or sanctioned by Yahweh, and it is Yahweh who gives the victory. Thus, we read in 1 Samuel chapter 17 verses 45–47 concerning the fight to the death between David and the Philistine Goliath:

Then David said to the Philistine, "You come to me with a sword and with a spear and with a javelin; but I come to you in the name of the Lord of hosts, the God of the armies of Israel, whom you have defied. This day the Lord will deliver you into my hand...for the battle is Yahweh's."

In holy war, there can be no question about ethics or morality. The prohibition against killing another human being is no longer valid because a higher divine order must now be followed. Because of the extreme, unconditional nature of holy war, it was imperative that the leaders verify in some way the will of the deity. For this purpose, dreams were interpreted (Judges 7.13–14), lots (Urim) were cast and prophets were consulted (1 Samuel 28.6). Just before the battle of Gilboa in which Saul was defeated by the Philistines and lost his life, he attempted in vain to verify the will of Yahweh. "When Saul saw the army of the Philistines, he was afraid, and his heart trembled greatly. And when Saul inquired of the Lord, the Lord did not answer him, either by dreams, or by Urim, or by prophets" (1 Samuel 28.6). Viewing the mighty army of the Philistines, Saul was terrified because he could not verify the will of the deity. If he were indeed about to lead his army into a holy war, the might of the Philistines would be irrelevant. In holy war, numbers and human strength did not matter because it was Yahweh who gave the victory. The religious character of the holy war is reflected further in the requirement of purity on the part of the soldiers. Contact with a bodily discharge contaminated a soldier and required purification, and sexual intercourse during the holy war was strictly prohibited. When holy war required the complete annihilation of the enemy, it is likely that the killing was understood as a form of sacrifice to the deity. At the battle of Jericho, Joshua said to the people: "Shout; for Yahweh has given you the city. And the city and all that is within it shall be devoted to Yahweh for destruction" (Joshua 6.16–17).

After the development of the monarchy in Israel, the understanding of war changed. The prophets who announced the divine sanction for war in this period were closely connected with the royal court, and warfare was transformed from a charismatic event to an instrument of national policy. Another radical change came with the fall of the Israelite kingdoms and the subsequent exiles. In the postexilic period, the only conceivable form of holy war was revolt against the ruling power of the day, whether it was against the Seleucids during the Maccabean Revolt or against the Romans during the Great Revolt of the first century and the Bar Kokhba Rebellion of the second century.

Although the Maccabean Revolt was successful, the destruction of the Temple under Emperor Vespasian in AD 70 and the devastation of Judea by Emperor Hadrian following the unsuccessful Bar Kokhba Revolt made a lasting impression on the rabbis of late antiquity and the Middle Ages. I am relying at this point on the research of Professor Reuven Firestone of Hebrew Union College.[12] I won't go into detail, but I can summarize his views in this way. In both the Jerusalem and the Babylonian Talmud, the rabbis interpreted the biblical text in such a way that holy war could no longer be *initiated*; holy wars in their original form were historically limited to the conquests of Joshua in response to the divine command. Admittedly, the Jerusalem Talmud allowed for a *defensive* holy war, but even this concession is absent in the Babylonian Talmud. In effect, the rabbis built a fence around the notion of holy war so that it became virtually unthinkable in their contemporary world. This was, in my opinion, a remarkable achievement of the rabbis.

The Just War

The notion of a just war is not a *religious* idea, but rather a *legal* one. If the concept of the *holy war* was developed in the Ancient Near East, the notion of a *just war* was a European development. To be more specific, the idea of a just war was conceived within the context of Roman law, and in the period of the late Roman Republic, Cicero discussed it in several of his works. In the early fifth century, the famous Christian theologian Augustine took over the idea from Cicero and passed it along to Thomas Aquinas in the thirteenth century. Today, the concept of a just war is a part of the official doctrine of the Roman Catholic Church and can be found in the Catholic Catechism in connection with the commandment: "You shall not kill". Within the context of Christianity, the idea of a just war did not remain, however, a purely legal notion, but rather it acquired an *ethical* dimension. The Catholic Catechism makes it quite clear that a just war is not only one that conforms to certain legal requirements. In addition, the just war is ethically defensible. As we shall see, it is the confusion of the legal with the ethical that causes problems for our thinking about this type of war.

Historical sources indicate that the notion of a just war developed very early in the history of Rome, going back perhaps to the seventh century BC during the reign of Hostilius (the third of the seven kings of Rome, reigning 673–642 BC).[13] To ensure that only just wars were fought, a collegium of priests was formed and entrusted with duties involving foreign affairs. The collegium was made up of approximately 20 members who were called "fetials" (from Latin: *fetiales*) and who were chosen from the upper class. Serving in this capacity lifelong, they gave advice on foreign affairs and international treaties; they were responsible for making proclamations of peace and war; and they traveled as ambassadors and had the authority to confirm treaties. In this way, the ultimate authority for declaring war was taken out of the hands of the king and bestowed upon a group of 20 men who were legally bound to follow certain procedures prior to any declaration of war. In theory, only wars of self-defense could possibly qualify as just wars.

A typical example would have been a foreign attack on Roman soil or an attack on a friendly Roman delegation outside of Roman territory. Should the king be convinced that Rome had suffered a grievance justifying a declaration of war, he was to submit his proposal to the collegium. The chief spokesman of the collegium, called the *pater patratus* ("executive father"), was the fetial priest whose duty it was to ratify treaties by means of religious rites. He together with a delegation from Rome would travel to the offending city in order to announce the grievance. Before crossing the boundary of the city, the spokesman would perform a ceremony in which the grievance would be proclaimed. After crossing over into the city, he would announce it a second time on the streets, a third time at the main city gate and a fourth time at the market place. If the city offered to negotiate and a settlement was reached, the matter was ended. If the city requested a period of deliberation, the spokesman would offer a maximum of 30 days. Should no resolution be found after 30 days, the spokesman of the collegium would threaten war and return to Rome where he would declare that the grievance had not been resolved and that a just war could be waged. The formal resolution to wage war would be made by the king and the senate on advice of the collegium. After the declaration of war, the chief spokesman of the collegium would return to the border of the offending city, throw a javelin dipped in blood across the boundary and verbally declare war. The entire process was bound by legal requirements, and, therefore, the chief spokesman invoked in his statements Jupiter, head of the Roman Pantheon, not Mars who was the god of war. The concern of the Romans was not that it be a *holy* war, but rather a *just* war, that is, a war that conformed to the necessary legal requirements.

As Rome developed its territory and its borders became wider and wider, the procedure of the collegium became from a practical standpoint impossible, and by the time of Cicero, it is clear that the procedure had become a mere formality. The Romans would force a prisoner of war to purchase a small plot of land within the city of Rome itself so that throwing the javelin onto this plot would fulfill the original requirement of traveling to the border of the offending city. Nevertheless, the Romans never admitted that they fought anything except just wars, just as they never admitted that they had abandoned the Republic and become an Empire.

The classic formulation of the concept of a just war is found in the writings of Thomas Aquinas. In his *Summa Theologiae*, he devotes several sections to the matter of war and begins by posing this question: "Whether waging war is always a sin." The very fact that the word "sin" appears in this context indicates the shift of emphasis from Cicero to Thomas Aquinas. For Cicero, the problem of a just war was primarily a legal and political matter; for Thomas Aquinas, it became a theological and an ethical matter. Is it possible to reconcile the notion of war with Christian teachings? In the end, Thomas Aquinas answers this question affirmatively, but he sets requirements for a just war that render it virtually impossible—an interesting parallel to the accomplishment of the medieval rabbis. The first two of these three requirements could conceivably be met; the war must be declared by a legitimate authority, and it must be declared for a just cause such as self-defense. The third requirement, however, addresses the *intention* of the war, which brings us into the realm of the psyche. What is the real motivation for declaring the war? If war is declared with the intention of promoting good or avoiding evil, then the requirement is fulfilled. If, on the other hand, the desire to dominate or to inflict cruel revenge is the motivation for declaring war, a just war is impossible even if the first two requirements are fulfilled. The modern Catechism of the Catholic Church has expanded the requirements of a just war, adding, for instance, a requirement regarding the humane treatment of civilians, wounded soldiers and prisoners of war. Furthermore, we read in the Catechism: "The strict conditions for legitimate defense by military force require rigorous consideration. The gravity of such a decision makes it subject to rigorous conditions of moral legitimacy." It is precisely this moral/ethical aspect that is characteristic of the modern concept of a just war and that distinguishes it from the purely legal understanding of the Roman Republic. When we speak today about a just war, we mean that it is ethically defensible.

The Honorable War

Like the just war of Cicero, the honorable war is not a religious concept. It differs, however, from the just war in that it is completely divorced from legal and ethical considerations. The honorable war is waged because it is a matter of *honor* to wage it.

There is in this case no appeal to a divine command and no attempt to justify the destruction of life. The waging of war as such is considered to be honorable. War is glorified because it is the means through which men fulfill their destiny, through which men become truly men. In order to exemplify this model of war, I turn back again to the Roman period, this time not to the period of the late Republic, but rather to the last century of the Western Roman Empire.

At the beginning of the fifth century, a man was born on the Great Hungarian Plain who decisively contributed to the fall of the Roman Empire in the West; he is known today as Attila the Hun.[14] At a famous battle in the Champagne region of France in June AD 451, the army of Attila the Hun clashed with the Romans and Goths in a fierce battle that lasted for several days. As the Hun army was being pushed back by the Romans and Goths, Attila is reported to have rallied his troops with these words:

> Huns, here you stand after victories over many nations and after conquering the world…For what is war to you but a way of life? What is more satisfying for a brave man than to seek revenge with his own hand? Nature imposes on us this heavy duty: to glut our souls with vengeance. Let us attack the enemy keenly, for those who press on with the battle are always bolder…Let the wounded claim in recompense the death of his opponent; let those who are unharmed, glory in the slaughter of the enemy…I shall throw the first spear at the foe. If any man can stand unmoved while Attila fights, then he must already be dead.[14(p247)]

Whether Attila actually uttered these words is uncertain, but as far as it can be determined from available sources, they are typical of his understanding of war: The waging of war is a matter of glory and honor.

The original home of the Huns cannot be determined with

certainty, but it is probable that they lived on the Central Asian Steppe, approximately the region of modern Kazakhstan between China and the Caspian Sea. Kazakhstan is geographically the ninth largest country in the world and at its center is the most extensive dry steppe region on earth, covering 300,000 square miles. The Huns were nomads, shepherds on horseback, who developed highly skilled techniques of warfare. They had no permanent settlements and were, therefore, dependent on regular contact with farmers and craftsmen on the more fertile edges of the steppe. The Huns had no infantry, but a cavalry that terrified even the Romans. The Huns could stay on horseback for days, and they became expert marksmen with the short bow while charging at full gallop. We don't know why the Huns left the Central Asian Steppe, but sometime in the second half of the fourth century, they began moving westward 700 miles through the Ukraine to Romania and finally onto the Great Hungarian Plain just north of the Danube, which was the boundary of the Western Roman Empire. Here Attila was born and from here the Huns began their attack on Europe.

On the Great Hungarian Plain, the Huns ceased to be nomads and built an unusual type of empire. As far as we can determine, their raids on villages and cities within the Roman Empire were never aimed at land acquisition. The Huns wanted the wealth of the land, not the land itself. The Huns were parasitic; they creamed off the wealth of the regions around them and consumed their food. They burned undefended farms and villages to the ground and sacked a long list of cities. The brutality and cruelty of the Huns together with the disorienting effect of their tactical methods made them the most feared group in the entire Roman Empire. War was a way of life for the Huns, and their only gain from their devastating raids was the acquisition of booty and the confirmation of their honor.

Many referred to them as the "wolves of the North", but the Huns were not simply wild savages. According to Christopher

Kelly, one of the leading authorities on the Huns, the young Attila spent most of his time in the company of his older brother Bleda. Together they were taught archery, how to fight with sword and lasso, and how to ride and care for a horse. Whether Attila could read is uncertain, but he certainly developed a mind for military tactics and for diplomatic negotiations. We have repeated examples of Attila negotiating terms with the Romans or the Goths before a surprise attack. The constant waging of war with its unspeakable devastation was not the result of their native savagery, but a necessary condition of leadership in Hun culture. Without the more permanent institution of kingship, there was no clear succession of leadership within the group. That meant that ambitious individuals could rapidly rise to prominence by demonstrating their courage and success in warfare. Only as long as a Hun leader was successful in warfare could he expect to rely on the loyalty of his followers. The Hun leader acquired honor and glory through warfare, not through the bloodline of a royal family. For this reason, the honorable war was a way of life for the Huns, and neither religious nor legal-ethical considerations had any place in this context.

If we reflect upon these three models of war in a contemporary setting, we will undoubtedly find the holy war to be the most radical and the most feared. A war that has the sanction of the divine has set aside temporarily all ethical and moral considerations. It is a matter of the cosmic struggle between good and evil, and the total victory of the good must be attained at all costs. One would think that this type of war would no longer be possible in a secularized world, but the events that have unfolded in recent years have demonstrated how resilient these primitive concepts really are. The good against the evil is probably the most powerful motive behind the slaughter of war. It justifies a clear separation between *us* and *them* and allows a dehumanization of them that renders murder a "morally good" act. With a strange twist of thought, we arrive at the following: We have not really *murdered* them, we have *saved* the world. The absoluteness of this mode of thinking presupposes that it is grounded in the Absolute, but any attempt to do this within the context of a religion such as Judaism, Christianity or Islam is doomed to failure in a secularized world. The result will necessarily be a radical religious fundamentalism that denies the reality of the world around it. In the end, the holy war is no longer "holy" in the historically relevant sense; it is simply radical.

If the holy war is *impossible* in the modern world, the honorable war would seem to be *unnecessary*. Then, the apparent necessity of the honorable war grew out of a situation in which the authority of the leader was constantly in question. Where there is no institutional structure guaranteeing the stability and succession of leadership, the authority of the leader must be reaffirmed continually through successes of some sort, and the demonstration of prowess in war has proven to be a powerful means of attaining this end. Given the complex structures of modern democracies, one would expect this type of war to have become obsolete. It is not necessary, for instance, for the President of the United States to demonstrate prowess in war in order to retain his office as President. Nevertheless, the element of honor in war has proven difficult to eliminate. Even if the Office of the President is not in question, there remains the matter of favorability among the public and the legacy to be left behind. Be that as it may, it is a fallacy to think that success in war can bolster the honor of a person who does not really participate in it. The days of Julius Caesar, Alexander the Great and Attila the Hun are past and gone; today's leaders do not risk their own lives and would be well advised to seek honor through diplomacy, rather than through war.

Given the difficulties of a holy war in a secular society and of an honorable war in a highly institutionalized society, the just war seems to provide the most plausible argument for making the step from murder to war, and in fact, it is precisely the just war that has received international attention and extensive debate. Even in cases where thoughts of a holy war or an honorable war are lurking beneath the surface, it is usually the just war that is openly discussed. Unless one wishes to adopt a consistently pacifist view of war, which I do not, one needs criteria for determining when a war is unavoidable and when it is not, and indeed the concept of a just war seems to provide the most promising basis for making such distinctions. Nevertheless, the ambiguity of the word "just" in the phrase "just war" should be resolved at the outset; by "just", we do not mean *morally acceptable*, but rather *legally conformant*. The only convincing argument for a war is, in my opinion, that it be declared (*ius ad bellum*) and conducted (*ius in bello*) according to internationally recognized legal standards. In declaring war, we acknowledge that these standards should also be applied against us, if the occasion arises. We further acknowledge that war is never morally justifiable; we enter into war with regret that it is apparently unavoidable in an imperfect world; and we are prepared to make reparation when it is over.

4

Why Is Darwin Still a Topic of Debate?

When we consider that it has been over 150 years since the publication of Darwin's groundbreaking work *On the Origin of Species*, we have to ask ourselves why the validity of his ideas is still a topic of discussion and sometimes heated debate. No one worries today about the discoveries of Kepler, Galileo or Newton, although the theories of these scientists brought about a revolution in our understanding of the physical world. But Darwin?! After he died, he was lucky to be placed in Westminster Abbey off to the side, as it were, in the shadow of the great Sir Isaac Newton. And even today, the creationists are still convinced that the theory of evolution is wrong. So we ask the question: What did Darwin say that was so disturbing?

You don't have to read much of the literature on Darwin and Darwinism to discover that the root problem for his critics has very little to do with *science* and very much to do with *religion* and *philosophy*. Darwin himself gives us a clue to this in a letter that he wrote to his friend Sir John Fordyce on 7 May 1879:

> It seems to me absurd to doubt that a man may be an ardent theist and an evolutionist...But as you ask, I may state that my judgment often fluctuates...In my most extreme fluctuations I have never been an Atheist in the sense of denying the existence of God. I think that generally (and more and more as I grow older), but not always, that an Agnostic would be the more correct description of my state of mind.[15(p190)]

In describing himself as an agnostic, Darwin implies that it is impossible to know, or better, to demonstrate in any convincing manner the existence of God. So our question now becomes:

What was it about his theory that rendered a demonstration of the existence of God impossible?

In order to answer this question, we have to place Darwin in the historical context of scientific development from the seventeenth to the nineteenth century. For simplicity, I focus on Galileo and Newton. Before the discoveries of Galileo, the Western world still held to the basic Aristotelian view of the physical universe. Everything in the region of our daily lives was thought to be composed of the four elements: earth, fire, air and water. In contrast, the moon and the heavenly bodies beyond it were thought to be composed of a fifth substance: the quintessence or ether. It was the substance of perfection, and the bodies composed of it had the geometric shape of perfection: the sphere. According to this view, there were several regions of the heavens ascending from the moon to the stars and finally to the highest region of the deity. Galileo destroyed this worldview of perfection by discovering among other things spots on the sun and mountains on the moon. So the inorganic world turned out to be less perfect than one had thought. Then, Newton developed in his *Principia Mathematica* the laws of force that describe the movement of objects on earth as well as in the heavens. Since the heavens obey the same physical laws as objects on earth, they could no longer be viewed as sacred. By the end of the eighteenth century, Newton's physics had been developed by other scientists such as Leonhard Euler and Joseph Louis Lagrange into a totally new worldview, a mechanical world where everything has a cause and an effect. In this world, there is no place for God to interact with humans; *the causal nexus is complete and exclusive.*

Christian theologians and philosophers alike responded to this new worldview by redefining their understanding of God's *action* in the world. Admittedly, God cannot break the causal chain of the physical world, but in order to avoid an infinite regress in the chain, it is necessary to posit a *first* cause and this is, so it was maintained, what we mean when we say the word

"God". God created the universe, set it in motion and then left it to operate on its own. The theologians and philosophers who maintained this view were called Deists (John Toland, Matthew Tindal and others).

It is important to note that this mechanical view of the world was only valid for the *inorganic* world. The *organic* world could not be explained on the principles of Newton. So the idea of life retained much of its old religious and philosophical significance, i.e. until the time of Darwin. Just as the pre-scientific inorganic world was thought to be hierarchical, the organic world was also thought to be hierarchical with humankind as the pinnacle. The notion of humankind as the top of the pyramid was supported biblically by the creation narrative in Genesis as well as in certain other passages such as Psalm 8, where we read: "Yet thou hast made him little less than God, and dost crown him with glory and honor. Thou hast given him dominion over the works of thy hands: thou hast put all things under his feet." And philosophically, the superiority of human beings was supported by the writings of Aristotle, especially his work on psychology entitled *Concerning the Soul*. According to Aristotle, only human beings have the capacity of reason, and therefore he defined a human as the "rational animal". Furthermore, the hierarchy of the organic world descending from humans to animals and finally to plants was considered to be stable and unchanging, and this idea of the constancy of the species was thoroughly consistent with the Newtonian mechanical universe, which was also unchanging. In fact, Newton's universe had no arrow of time; it was Darwin, not Newton, who introduced the concept of dynamic process into science. The process of evolution is dynamic and has a temporal direction. This seems, of course, very commonsense. After all, young people get older; old people don't get younger. But this direction of movement was unknown in Newtonian physics.

Returning to our hierarchical view of life, the fact that the laws of Newton did not apply to the organic world encouraged theologians of the Anglican Church to focus on life as evidence of the existence of God. Foremost among these Anglican theologians was William Paley (born 1743) who published in 1802 his classic work *Natural Theology or Evidences of the Existence and Attributes of the Deity*. This book became a standard textbook in Christ's College in Cambridge where Charles Darwin studied theology, and when Darwin took his theological exams in 1831, he was tested on the theology of William Paley. So if we want to understand how Darwin in his early years understood God in relation to life, we have to read Paley's theology, where we find the classic argument for the existence of God: the Watchmaker. Paley writes:

In crossing a heath, suppose I pitched my foot against a *stone*, and were asked how the stone came to be there, I might possibly answer, that for any thing I knew to the contrary, it had lain there forever; nor would it perhaps be very easy to shew the absurdity of this answer. But suppose I had found a *watch* upon the ground, and it should be enquired how the watch happened to be in that place, I should hardly think of the answer which I had before given, that, for any thing I knew, the watch might have always been there. Yet, why should not this answer serve for the watch, as well as for the stone? Why is it not as admissible in the second case, as in the first? For this reason, and for no other, viz. that, when we come to inspect the watch, we perceive (what we could not discover in the stone) that its several parts are framed and put together for a purpose...This mechanism being observed (it requires indeed an examination of the instrument, and perhaps some previous knowledge of the subject, to perceive and understand it; but being once, as we have said, observed and understood,) the inference, we think, is inevitable; that the watch must have had a maker; that there must have existed, at some time and at some place or other, an artificer or artificers who formed it for the purpose, which we find it actually to answer; who comprehended its construction, and designed its use.[16(p7f)]

Applying the analogy of the watch and the watchmaker to the organic world, Paley presents an argument for the existence of God based on design. Because we observe order and design in the world, particularly in the organic world, we can reasonably infer that there was a being who designed it. Where there's a watch, there must be a watchmaker; where there's design, there must be a designer. Consider, for example, the birds in a particular area. We note that the length of their beaks is well suited to the area in which they live; such design—and hence the existence of a designer—is, according to Paley, irrefutable. To anticipate a bit: It was exactly this argument that Darwin rendered untenable, and without this argument there was in his mind no way to know whether or not God existed.

Charles Darwin was not the first person to develop a theory of evolution; he was not even the first *Darwin* to develop the idea of evolution. His paternal grandfather Erasmus Darwin, a physician and poet, had developed his own theory of evolution and in a poem published posthumously, he speculated that life originated in the sea. Yet, more important than Erasmus Darwin was his contemporary Jean Baptiste Lamarck, the French naturalist, who developed a theory of evolution based on the idea of a life force driving the whole process toward some goal (*telos*). According to Lamarck, organisms adapt to their environment and pass on the acquired adaptive features to the next generation. His classic example was the giraffe, which stretched its neck to reach the higher branches for food and passed this acquired adaptive feature on to the next generation. Then, there was the British philosopher Herbert Spencer who actually coined the phrase "survival of the fittest", which incidentally does not appear in Darwin's first edition of *On the*

Origin of Species. So the idea of the evolution of life forms was current at the time of Darwin, but no one before Darwin had developed a scientific theory based on *empirical* evidence.

The influences on Darwin and his theory were numerous. We have just mentioned his grandfather Erasmus Darwin, Jean Baptiste Lamarck and Herbert Spencer. In addition, there was Thomas Malthus, the English economist, who developed a population theory according to which the human population of the earth develops at a geometrical rate. In *On the Origin of Species*, Darwin actually mentions this theory explicitly. On the other hand, the empirical data came from the famous voyage to South America with Captain Robert FitzRoy of the Royal Navy on HMS *Beagle*, a voyage that lasted four years and nine months and that allowed Darwin to collect extremely valuable specimens and to produce literally thousands of pages of geological and zoological notes. The history of science would be different, had Darwin not made this voyage, and as his biographers report, he almost didn't make it. At this point in the narrative, we come to speak about Darwin's family, which was in many ways very influential in his life.

Darwin was born in 1809 into a very well-to-do Victorian family. Both his father and his paternal grandfather were well-known physicians, and his maternal grandfather Josiah Wedgwood was the founder and owner of the famous Wedgwood pottery company. So Charles' mother was a Wedgwood, and when Charles married, he married his cousin Emma Wedgwood, thus securing a double inheritance from the Wedgwood fortune. In addition, his father Dr Robert Darwin was a shrewd investor and assisted Charles in several financial ventures. In sum, Charles Darwin not only belonged to the middle-upper class of Victorian society, he was also one of the financial beneficiaries of the industrial revolution in England of the nineteenth century.

In accordance with the wishes of his father, Charles went to

Edinburgh in 1825 to study medicine, but after two years, it was apparent that he was ill suited for the medical profession. With a considerable degree of disappointment, Dr Robert Darwin suggested that Charles leave Edinburgh and move to Cambridge where he was to study theology at Christ's College. In 1831, Charles completed his exams and shortly thereafter received the invitation to accompany Captain FitzRoy. Darwin's father, however, was totally opposed to the venture and insisted that Charles should take over a parish and pursue a career as a clergyman in the Anglican Church. At this point, Josiah Wedgwood intervened on Charles' behalf and convinced Robert that the voyage would be good experience for Charles. So the historic voyage took place, and Darwin collected the necessary empirical data for his theory.

Josiah Wedgwood's influence on Charles' life went well beyond securing the permission of Robert Darwin for the famous voyage with Captain FitzRoy. Charles held his grandfather in great esteem and saw in the competition of the free market a parallel to the struggle for existence in nature. The companies that could adapt to their surroundings and find a niche in the market survived; the ones that couldn't adapt eventually failed. So with the voluminous data from the voyage, with the knowledge of Lamarck's evolutionary theory and Malthus' population theory, against the background of philosophical ideas such as those of Herbert Spencer and with a clear grasp of the functioning of capitalist free markets, Charles Darwin developed a theory of evolution that in its basic concepts is still valid today.

Without going into detail, we can say that the two main ideas of Darwin's theory are *variation* and *natural selection*. As an illustration, consider a particular species of birds. Individual birds in one generation reproduce birds in the next generation that are not exact copies of their parents. That is, certain variations occur in the next generation—say, for instance, the length of the beak— that help these birds adapt to their surroundings and survive. If birds with shorter beaks miss out and fail to find food, they will not reproduce and leave descendants. The birds with longer beaks will be able to survive and reproduce so that the third generation will also have longer beaks. Note that the competition is within the same species. The individuals of the species are competing in the same area for the same food and for a mate of the same species in order to reproduce. Just as a cell-phone company doesn't compete with a fast-food company, birds don't compete with elephants. Over a long period of time, the process of natural selection based on the competitive advantage of certain variations produces new species.

That Darwin's theory of evolution hit the nerve of the Anglican Church was apparent shortly after the publication of *On the Origin of Species* in 1859 and was epitomized in the famous debate between Thomas Huxley and Bishop Samuel Wilberforce at the University of Oxford in 1860. Although this debate is an interesting topic in itself, it is not very helpful in clarifying our problem: What was it about Darwin's theory that rendered a demonstration of the existence of God impossible? As we have seen, the chief argument for the existence of God in the Anglican Church was the argument from design. The order and design of the organic world point to a creator. Darwin agrees that there is a certain order in the organic world, but from this fact, he draws a different conclusion. He says in effect: "Yes, we see order in the universe. The birds in this area have nice long beaks so that they can obtain the necessary food for their survival. But the reason that we observe these birds with nice long beaks is because all of the short-beaked birds died out! It's not because a supreme being designed it this way. It's because only those individuals survive that fit their environment." *Voilà!* There we have a perfectly reasonable scientific explanation for the orderliness of nature, leaving us unsure whether we are observing any real design or just plain biological accident. And if the species that we observe today are really just the outcome of a long series of biological accidents, how can we seriously talk about the dignity of humankind? In one fell swoop, Darwin dismantled two of the most important ideas of the Anglican Church: the design argument for the existence of God and the dignity of humankind as the pinnacle of creation.

After the publication of *On the Origin of Species*, Darwin received enormous criticism not only from theologians of the Anglican Church, but also from fellow scientists. There were two problems that he could not solve. First of all, without a knowledge of genetics, he could not explain how the variations occur. In 1868, he published a second book entitled *Variation*, in which he proposed the notion of "pangenesis"; according to this hypothesis, the offspring of two parents should be a fifty percent mixture of each parent. Nobody was very impressed with the idea, and in fact, the hypothesis proved to be totally wrong. During Darwin's lifetime, Georg Mendel, a curious Augustinian monk living in what is today the Czech Republic, had done work on genetics, crossing yellow and green peas, but to my knowledge, Darwin was unaware of Mendel's work. Not until the discovery of DNA in 1953 was it really clear how the variations occur. Secondly, the process of evolution is a very, very, very slow process. In order for the process of variation and natural selection to produce an organism such as a human being, billions of years (about 3.5 to be more exact) are required, and during Darwin's lifetime, nobody would have dreamed that the earth had been in existence for this length of time. Even the most liberal geologists were only thinking in terms of about 75,000 years, and there were still well-known geologists who were holding to the 6000-year figure of Archbishop James Ussher of Ireland. In his famous *Sacred Chronology* of 1620, Ussher had determined that the creation of the world must have begun on 23 October 4004 BC. So the accepted age of the earth did not allow for the evolution of organisms as Darwin conceived it.

On reading *On the Origin of Species*, one is struck by the fact that Darwin does not discuss the descent of humankind. To be sure, there are plenty of conclusions that one can draw about the evolution of human beings, but his explicit treatment of the matter came later in the publication of *The Descent of Man* in 1871. Contrary to popular belief, Darwin did not suggest that human beings descended from apes, but rather that humans and apes have a common ancestor in the tree of evolution. What was damaging to the dignity of humankind was Darwin's assertion that there is no essential difference between human beings and animals—a point that he makes quite clear in his discussion of conscience. In Chapter 3, Darwin writes:

> I fully subscribe to the judgment of those writers who maintain that of all the differences between man and the lower animals, the moral sense or conscience is by far the most important...The following proposition seems to me in a high degree probable—namely, that any animal whatever, endowed with well-marked social instincts, would inevitably acquire a moral sense or conscience, as soon as its intellectual powers had become as well developed, or nearly as well developed, as in man.[17(p70–72)]

There is, therefore, no qualitative difference between human beings and animals. From this standpoint, it becomes clear that Darwin was not a humanist in any meaningful sense since the humanist tradition stemming from the Renaissance recognized above all things the dignity of humankind and the special position of human beings in the order of nature and history.

There is a deep irony in the way in which Darwin's theory of evolution has been received in the United States. Although significant portions of the population still reject the idea of evolution, Darwin's ideas of variation, selection, competition and survival of the fittest have been wholeheartedly received as a political and economic philosophy. In the writings of the great industrialist

Andrew Carnegie, we see the beginning of a "Corporate Darwinism" that still drives American business today. In an article published in 1889 in the *North American Review* entitled "Wealth" Carnegie writes:

> The price which society pays for the law of competition...is...great; but the advantages of this law are also greater still, for it is to this law that we owe our wonderful material development...But, whether the law be benign or not, we must say of it...It is here; we cannot evade it; no substitutes for it have been found; and while the law may be sometimes hard for the individual, it is best for the race, because it insures the survival of the fittest in every department.[18(p655)]

This article appeared again in Carnegie's book *The Gospel of Wealth* (1901). Since the time of the great industrialists like Carnegie, there have been numerous books written on Corporate or Business Darwinism, but the message from Carnegie down to Carly Fiorina who often quoted Darwin is clear: "We don't have to worry about the short-beaked birds. They will die out, and we will survive. The individual may suffer, but the race will prosper." Through the development of social Darwinism in Germany—primarily through the writings of Ernst Haeckel, a German contemporary of Darwin—this type of thinking found its way into the Third Reich and led to consequences that are all too familiar to us today. Much like Ayn Rand, the Russian immigrant who has been praised by Alan Greenspan, Ernst Haeckel developed a philosophy that made a virtue of selfishness. Charles Darwin himself was vehemently opposed to expanding the theory of evolution beyond the biological realm. The fact that religious conservatives can reject Darwin's theory of evolution in the *biological realm*, while adopting the substance of the theory in the *political* and *economic* realm, is nothing less than a deep contradiction in American culture—one that has potentially dangerous consequences.

When we posed our original question: What did Darwin say that was so disturbing?, we were considering only the debate instigated by the conservatives over creationism. To our surprise, however, we have arrived at a two-pronged answer that is directed toward both conservatives and liberals. Darwin's theory of evolution was disturbing to conservatives because it offered a convincing scientific explanation for order and design in the organic world and dethroned human beings from the pinnacle of an organic hierarchy. In the form of social Darwinism, his theory has proven to be disturbing to liberals because it has provided a quasi-scientific basis for the cruelty of the business world and for the corporate plundering of the economy. If we could end the fruitless debate between the creationists and the evolutionists and if we could recognize the fundamental error of applying evolutionary concepts to the social and business spheres, we might benefit more in our everyday lives from the work of Charles Darwin. Then, Darwin's theory places all of us before the broader question of the meaning of life. If we are just accidents of a long process of evolution, does life ultimately have any real meaning? It is at this point that the religious discussion should begin.

5

Virgin Births and Linguistic Events

While driving through the Villages where I live, I have seen a bumper sticker that reads: "Keep Christ in Christmas". Like most bumper stickers, it's very cryptic. What does that mean: "Keep Christ in Christmas"? At first glance, one is inclined to disregard it—not only because it's cryptic, but also because it sounds so trivial. But then, every bumper sticker strikes me as trivial; there is, after all, a certain trivializing effect of posting a message directly above a metal pipe that emits poisonous gas. Still, communication through bumper stickers seems to be a cultural phenomenon in the US, and so I can't resist asking myself what this person is trying to communicate. It's as though the person makes a cryptic statement about something he considers important and then hastens away before anyone can ask any questions. So if I happen to be following this car down a boulevard, I find myself trying to decipher the message: "Keep Christ in Christmas". Since the owner of the car apparently has no intention of explaining it to me, I take my first hint from the visual image; the sticker looks like a little nativity scene with the customary manger, a baby and two people standing around. So the message must be: Keep in mind at Christmas time that Jesus was born in a stable and placed in a manger.

I am not sure, however, that focusing our attention on the manger is a particularly good idea. Out of all the writers of the New Testament, Luke is the only one who seems to know anything about a manger (Luke 2.7,12 and 16). Matthew reports that Jesus was born in a house; Mark and John, for their part, don't seem to care where he was born. If I could speak to the owner of this sticker, he would perhaps tell me that I am missing the point. The nativity scene is meant to communicate something else, namely, that Jesus was born in a humble, but miraculous way. To be more specific, Jesus was born of the Virgin Mary, with the emphasis on "virgin", not on "Mary". So it really doesn't matter if Matthew reports the birth of Jesus as taking place in a house, and Luke places it in a stable because there was no room in the inn. It doesn't matter that Luke talks about shepherds, whereas Matthew reports only the wise men. As the early Christian creeds did, we can overlook all such inconsistencies in the details and focus on the miraculous virgin birth. In the Apostles' Creed we read, for instance: "I believe in Jesus Christ, his only Son, our Lord, who was conceived by the Holy Spirit, born of the Virgin Mary." In view of this, "Keep Christ in Christmas" would mean: "Keep in mind the miracle of Christmas, that is, the virgin birth of Jesus Christ."

There are, however, three problems with this statement that we cannot avoid; the first is scientific, the second is literary and the third is historical. The scientific problem can be stated rather succinctly: Virgins don't have babies. There have been numerous attempts to explain how a virgin birth might have occurred, but in the end all such explanations remain in the region of fantasy. There are apparently rare cases of female dolphins or sharks that have become pregnant without male assistance, and from these cases the proponents of virgin birth have extrapolated to humans, arguing that Mary really could have been a virgin when Jesus was born. With the rise of modern genetics, the arguments have become more sophisticated in an attempt to show how the Virgin Mary could have given Jesus a Y chromosome. An interesting twist to this line of reasoning is the fascination of some feminists with the possibility of becoming mothers without the bother of dealing with men. Aarathi Prasad writes in the *Guardian*'s "Notes and Theories" blog: "What would it be like if women could have babies on their own? As a single mother, I thought it would be fabulous to have the option of another child without first having to find the right man."[19] Prasad postulates that Mary had a rare condition called testicular feminization, which means that she had an X and a Y chromosome. How this condition would enable a "virgin" birth remains, however, a matter of speculation.

The second problem is of a literary nature. The New Testament is not *one* book, but a collection of 27 books of varying length and content. Of these 27 books, there are only two that deemed it important to report the birth of Jesus at all: Matthew and Luke. Outside of these two books, there is absolutely no indication that Jesus was born of a virgin. The Apostle Paul, for instance, knew nothing about it; he assumed that Jesus had a perfectly normal birth. And even within the book of Matthew where the virgin birth is reported, it doesn't have the prominence that it has been assigned in the later creeds. If you open the book of Matthew and start reading the first chapter, you find a long genealogy that is intended to demonstrate the relationship between David and Jesus: "The book of the genealogy of Jesus Christ, the son of David, the son of Abraham...and Jacob the father of Joseph the husband of Mary, of whom Jesus was born..." Now if Joseph had *not* been the biological father, what possible sense could the genealogy have? The lineage from King David to Jesus is only meaningful on the assumption of a natural birth.

The third problem leads us beyond the bounds of the first-century Jewish community back to ancient Egypt of the third and second millennium BC. It is well known that the ancient Egyptians regarded their Pharaohs in some sense as divine. It is, however, less well known that the Pharaohs were thought to have been born of virgins. The virgin birth of the Pharaoh was an important element of Egyptian religion and was presented not only in written birth narratives, but also in graphic art of the period.[20] According to the mythology of the Egyptians, the spirit god Amun would approach the designated virgin and beget the future god-king of Egypt. The blessed virgin had to be newly married, but still a virgin, and the god Amun would announce the name to be given to the child. The mythological account of the virgin birth is attested in the literature of the second millennium, but it reflects a tradition that dates back to the third millennium BC. Had this tradition remained in Egypt, it might never have reappeared in the books of Matthew and Luke in the New Testament. But the expansion of the Greek Empire under Alexander the Great beginning in 334 BC and the ensuing cultural exchange of the Hellenistic Period down to 30 BC allowed the myth of the virgin birth to spread from Egypt to Greece and Palestine. Thus, we find in Athens a legend arising that Plato was born of a virgin. The god Apollo sent instruction to Ariston, the husband of Plato's mother, not to touch his virgin wife until after the birth of Plato. And according to Plutarch, the Greek historian of the first century AD, Alexander the Great himself was born of a virgin.

Since the story of the virgin birth was well established in the eastern Mediterranean region, it should not surprise us to see it appearing in two books of the New Testament. It is clearly mythological, but being mythological does not deprive it of meaning. Mythology is not meaningless; it's simply not historical in the modern sense. Mythology typically tries to give expression to something that is difficult to convey in prose or poetry. It tries to capture the incomprehensible in a language that doesn't belong to our world. In mythology, the gods interact with human beings as though they themselves had human characteristics. They walk, talk, express their feelings, become angry, and exercise their power by rewarding and punishing humans. A myth can be relatively simple or very elaborate, but in any case, a meaningful myth conceals an *existential concern*, which the author cannot express in ordinary language. To put it another way: *In a culture that thinks mythologically, existential concerns can only be expressed in mythological form.* So our task now becomes one of interpretation on two levels. We need to inquire about the *intention* of the virgin-birth narrative in general, and we need to inquire more specifically about its intention in the *New Testament*. The first question is easier to answer. In every known case of the virgin-birth myth in the ancient world, the intention was to emphasize the importance of the person under consideration. The Pharaohs were great rulers, and their greatness was foreshadowed by the manner of their birth. Plato was a man of extraordinary intelligence and wisdom, and his greatness was foreshadowed by the manner of his birth. Alexander the Great was a military leader of unequaled ability, building in a relatively short time an empire that extended eastward all the way to India. So again: His greatness was foreshadowed in the manner of his birth.

If the writer of Matthew chose to report the virgin birth of Jesus, he was obviously trying to emphasize the importance of Jesus in some way. Jesus was not, however, a great ruler nor was he a great writer like Plato. So the question remains: What was so outstanding about him that Matthew brings in the myth of the virgin birth? The answer to this question has to do with language. Put succinctly: Jesus was a "linguistic event" of the first order, and his virgin birth prepares us for what is to follow. At first glance, it might be surprising that I am focusing now on language. Let me explain the reason for this. In spite of what Mel Gibson thought, it is historically impossible to write a biography of Jesus. The necessary information is simply not available. Throughout the nineteenth century, competent historians and theologians sifted through the available biblical and extra-biblical material in an attempt to write "The Life of Jesus", but by the end of the century, the failure of the project was apparent to everyone. The whole matter was summed up in a classic work by Albert Schweitzer, *The Quest of the Historical Jesus*, which appeared originally in German under the title *Von Reimarus zu Wrede* (1906). When we bracket out the mythological and legendary elements of the New Testament, we are left with very little reliable historical information. We simply don't know a great deal about this man's life. If you are a biographer, that's very disappointing. But if you are a theologian, that's extremely interesting because it focuses your attention on the *message*, not the *messenger*. The historically most reliable information in the New Testament concerns the message of Jesus; it was his *word*, not his *person*, that the writers found to be of ultimate significance. So when Matthew reports the virgin birth, he is emphasizing what is about to follow: a message of such depth and power that it could no sooner be removed from the face of the earth than the words of Socrates. After the introductory portion of his book, Matthew reports the first great speech of Jesus, which is called the "Sermon on the Mount". "Blessed are the poor in spirit...Blessed are the peacemakers." These are truly remarkable statements. Then follow a radical interpretation of the law, a new understanding of prayer, a critique of wealth and so forth. At the conclusion of the speech, Matthew reports that the words of Jesus had an astonishing authority. In philosophical terms, we would say: These words of Jesus formed a *linguistic event*. And since linguistic events cannot be written, but only spoken, Jesus himself never committed a word of his message to written form. We can write *about* linguistic events, but the event itself *as* event must occur in the act of speaking.

Let me give a few examples. By way of comparison, I start with statements that do not qualify as linguistic events. The statement "It is cold in this room" conveys information, but it is not an event. "I have lived in the Villages for two years" also conveys information. Most statements in everyday conversation are of this type. They communicate a certain content, they give information about a thing or a situation and so forth. There is, however, a different class of statements that we call linguistic events because the *content* of the statement is *actualized in the speaking* of the statement. What the statement *says* actually *occurs* when it is spoken. A prime example of this occurs between two people when the words are spoken: "I love you." Imagine a romantic dinner by candlelight. It's the anniversary of the couple, and as they lift their wine glasses to toast, the words are spoken: "I love you." Nobody will understand this statement as purely a matter of information. In the very speaking of the words, the love is communicated. What the statement says actually occurs in the speaking. That's a linguistic event. There are, of course, other types of linguistic events that are less romantic. In general, this category includes commands, decrees, promises, insults and others. If I say to the host of a meeting: "I promise to give a shorter talk next time", the sentence does not simply convey information. The promise occurs in the statement itself. Or if I say to someone: "You're an absolute idiot", I am not simply providing an opinion or communicating information. I am insulting the person, and the insult occurs in the act of speaking itself. Verdicts in a courtroom are similar. When the judge pronounces the verdict, something occurs in the speaking that alters the life of the person charged. Linguistic events have a wide range of importance in our lives. Some are relatively insignificant; others literally change the course of our lives. The linguistic events that occurred through the words of Jesus were apparently of the latter type.

It was the depth and power of Jesus' words that created the aura around him. Some linguistic events that occurred in his speaking were simple; others were complex. When he said, for example: "Your sins are forgiven", and the hearer actually experienced the release from guilt in the act of his speaking, the occurrence was what I would call a simple linguistic event. The parables, on the other hand, built complex events going beyond the simple one-sentence events that we have been discussing. When he told the parable of the "Good Samaritan", something happened to the listeners. It was not just an interesting moral story that they were hearing. If only for a moment, they experienced what the parable said—a world in which there is a sponta-

Citizens of the Broken Compass

neous and natural concern of one human being for another, in which ethnic differences become unimportant, in which proper papers and credentials don't matter.

So significant were such linguistic events in the life of Jesus that the writer of the Gospel of John dispenses with the birth narrative altogether and focuses his attention totally on language. "In the beginning was the Word, and the Word was with God, and the Word was divine...And the Word became flesh and dwelt among us, full of grace and truth." That the words of Jesus were life-changing linguistic events is expressed here in the phrase "full of grace and truth". Admittedly, these biblical words are not our words, and they seem strange to our ears. We would be more inclined to say: "full of acceptance and authenticity". The words of Jesus, his sayings and parables, were expressions of acceptance and authenticity. He showed no particular preference for this or that person. He would talk to anybody. And he apparently did not care very much what a person had done before he met him; everything depended on whether the person would accept being accepted, whether the person could experience the alternative world of the parable, whether the person realized that the parables express life in its most authentic form.

There was another Jewish thinker who had similar ideas about parables. In a short piece entitled "On Parables" Franz Kafka writes:

Many complain that the words of the wise are always merely parables and of no use in daily life, which is the only life we have. When the sage says: "Go over," he does not mean that we should cross over to some actual place, which we could do anyhow if the labor were worth it; he means some fabulous yonder, something unknown to us, something too that he cannot designate more precisely, and therefore cannot help us here in the very least. And these parables really set out to say merely that the incomprehensible is incomprehensible, and

66

we know that already. But the cares we have to struggle with every day: that is a different matter.

Concerning this, a man once said: "Why such reluctance? If you only followed the parables, you yourselves would become parables and with that rid of all your daily cares."

Another said: "I bet that is also a parable."

The first said: "You have won."

The second said: "But unfortunately only in parable."

The first said: "No, in reality; in parable you have lost."[21]

Kafka suggests that we become parables, that we break the hold of everyday reality over our lives, that we adopt an alternative vision of life—a vision of a life no longer dominated by anxiety and worry. The questioner in Kafka's parable could not free himself from the illusion that the reality of everyday life is the only reality there is. He was comfortable in his logic about reality, and in reality, he won the argument. But he lost the parable; he lost the vision of something better, something beyond the everyday reality that we know. Indeed, it is difficult to find a more profound statement about parables than this: "If you only followed the parables, you yourselves would become parables and with that rid of all your daily cares."

The parables of Jesus were not just interesting little stories or moral lessons, but rather they were in the truest sense complex linguistic events. The listeners actually experienced what the parable said. For a brief moment, they lived in the parable, experiencing it as the most authentic form of life. Such linguistic events are spoken, not written. It is no accident that Jesus never wrote a word; the power of his message was in the speaking.

After his death, his followers were faced with the problem of transmitting that which could not be transmitted in written form. In order to indicate the power and depth of the linguistic events that they had experienced, they resorted to myth and legend. Jesus walked on water, he was born of a virgin and so forth.

These are not literary devices that we would use today. We can, however, appreciate the fact that they had their place in the Near Eastern culture of the first century. Through the myth of the virgin birth, Matthew emphasizes the power of the linguistic events that occurred in the language of Jesus. Over and over again, Matthew reports that Jesus spoke with an uncanny authority; the Greek word (*exusia*) that he uses also means "power". And remarkable as it may seem, the power of these linguistic events has helped to shape Western civilization.

"Keep Christ in Christmas" becomes then: "Let us keep in mind these linguistic events." They are in the long run more powerful than the sword. Should peace on earth ever become a reality, it will occur through events of language, not through acts of violence. Violence only destroys the body; language changes the heart. In a world in which violence has become the norm, that's worth remembering at Christmas time. *Violence destroys the body; language changes the heart.* Remembering this would give real substance to the phrase: "Keep Christ in Christmas".

6

Physics, Religion and Natural Law

There is a commonly expressed opinion about the relationship between science and religion in the seventeenth century. It goes something like this: Until the advent of classical physics in the seventeenth century, physical events in the world such as devastating storms, particularly good harvests or the appearance of comets in the sky were interpreted as the result of divine intervention. The laws of physics, however, rendered such explanations superfluous. In this regard, one thinks often of the famous three laws of motion developed by Sir Isaac Newton and presented in his *Principia Mathematica* (1687). Having acquired the knowledge of these laws, intelligent people of the seventeenth century no longer needed the notion of divine intervention in order to explain the world around them. In one fell swoop, human history moved from *religion* to *science*, from mythological explanations based on *tradition* to scientific explanations based on *experience and reason*. However, this picture of the seventeenth century is a gross oversimplification.

First of all, Newton did not develop the three laws of motion in quite the neat form in which we find them in modern textbooks on physics. He wrote his opus magnum not in English, but in Latin, and nowhere in this groundbreaking work do we find, for instance, the well-known equation $F = ma$. In fact, Newton's understanding of force was different from that found in our textbooks. Whereas he defined force in his second law as the change in impulse ($\Delta[m \cdot v]$), our standard textbooks define force as the change of impulse pro unit of time ($\Delta[m \cdot v]/\Delta t$ or simply ma). Furthermore, Newton was not totally clear on the meaning of the word "force", as Max Jammer notes in his detailed analysis of the concept of force in physics. Jammer writes: "it is obvious that the second law of motion was not intended by Newton as a definition of force...Force, for Newton, was a concept given a priori, intuitively, and ultimately in analogy to human muscular force".[22(p124)] Finally, Newton never asserted that the physical laws of nature render divine intervention superfluous. On the contrary, he considered that divine intervention was occasionally necessary in order to preserve the proper motion of the heavenly bodies. In particular, there were two points at which Newton viewed divine intervention as necessary: to prevent the fixed stars from falling together as a result of gravitational force and to adjust the deviations of the planets from their normal course, which was also caused by gravitational pull. In his *Opticks* (1704), Newton writes:

For while comets move in very excentrick orbs in all manner of positions, blind Fate could never make all the planets move one and the same way in orbs concentrick, some inconsiderable irregularities excepted, which may have risen from the mutual actions of comets and planets upon one another, and which will be apt to increase, till this system wants a reformation. Such a wonderful uniformity in the planetary system must be allowed the effect of choice.[23(p261-262)]

And further:

(God is) a powerful ever-living Agent; who being in all places, is more able by his will to move the bodies within his boundless uniform sensorium, and thereby to form and reform the parts of the universe, than we are by our will to move the parts of our own bodies.[23(p262)]

When the system of the planets requires a "reformation", a correction, the will of God moves the heavenly bodies into their proper positions. Alongside the laws of nature, Newton saw the necessity of "the effect of (God's) choice". This explains why one of Newton's preferred designations for God was "Pantokrator" ("the Almighty"). After Newton died, unpublished commentaries were discovered that he had written on the biblical books Daniel and Revelation, both highly apocalyptic writings.

It would be a mistake to think that Newton was an exception to the scientific climate of seventeenth-century England. Historical studies of this period have made it abundantly clear that the primary representatives of the new science in England were devout Puritans. I will not go into the reasons for this, but only note that 42 of the 87 members of the Royal Society in 1663, for whom biographical information is available, were professed Puritans. Perhaps no one represented the new scientific-puritanical attitude better than Robert Boyle who was one of the founders of the Royal Society in 1645. In his last will and testament, Boyle provided for an annual series of lectures known as the "Boyle Lectures", the expressed purpose of which was: "for proving the Christian religion against notorious Infidels".

If Isaac Newton was the scientific genius of the seventeenth century, Albert Einstein held that position of high regard in the twentieth century. After completing his study of physics in Zurich, Switzerland at the ETH (Swiss Federal Institute of Technology), Einstein took a job working in the patent office in the city of Bern, not being able at that time to secure a teaching position. While working in Bern, he published in 1905 one of the most significant articles in the history of physics: his article on the Special Theory of Relativity. The relativity of time and space as well as the equivalence of mass and energy ($E = mc^2$) pointed toward a deep connectivity in nature, and in Einstein's General Theory of Relativity, published in 1915, the interrelatedness of the time-space-continuum and mass was worked out in detail. What Newton had done for the seventeenth century, Einstein accomplished for the twentieth century. Newton had developed groundbreaking ideas about absolute time and absolute space;

Einstein gave physics a new foundation by developing the ideas of relative time and relative space. The parallel between Newton and Einstein extends, however, beyond the realm of science. Both men were deeply concerned about religious questions.

The most frequently quoted remark of Einstein regarding religion was made in 1940 at the Conference on Science, Philosophy, and Religion held at Union Theological Seminary in New York. On this occasion Einstein said: "Science without religion is lame, religion without science is blind." During the period from 1930 to 1940, Einstein published three important articles on science and religion. In the first of these articles, entitled "The World as I See It" (1930), Einstein made it clear that he could not conceive of a personal God in the traditional sense:

> I cannot conceive of a God who rewards and punishes his creatures, or has a will of the kind that we experience in ourselves. Neither can I nor would I want to conceive of an individual that survives his physical death...I am satisfied with the mystery of the eternity of life and with the awareness and a glimpse of the marvelous structure of the existing world, together with the devoted striving to comprehend a portion, be it ever so tiny, of the Reason that manifests itself in nature.[24(p8)]

Neither the Jewish nor the Christian understanding of God was acceptable to Einstein because he deplored all anthropomorphic ideas about God. For him, the experience of the mystery of nature was the source of all religious experience. Thus, he wrote in his article "Religion and Science" (1930): "The individual feels the futility of human desires and aims and the sublimity and marvelous order which reveal themselves both in nature and in the world of thought. Individual existence impresses him as a sort of prison and he wants to experience the universe as a single significant whole."[24(p38)] This experience of a single significant whole, of the deep rationality of the universe, Einstein describes as the cosmic religious experience:

> I maintain that the cosmic religious feeling is the strongest and noblest motive for scientific research...What a deep conviction of the rationality of the universe and what a yearning to understand...Kepler and Newton must have had to enable them to spend years of solitary labor in disentangling the principles of celestial mechanics![24(p39)]

Some readers of Einstein's articles have concluded that he was a mystic of sorts, but he himself rejected this designation in clear terms years after the aforementioned articles were written. In truth, Einstein's thoughts about religion are more closely related to the rationalism of philosophers like Spinoza than to any form of Eastern or Western mysticism.

Later physicists, particularly those who were actively involved in quantum physics research, have been much less cautious than Einstein about the possibility of mystical experience. Fritjof Capra, the particle physicist who taught at UC Berkeley, is well known for his book *The Tao of Physics*, but he has also written numerous other books in which he maintains that there are fundamental parallels between Eastern mysticism and quantum physics and that both are essential to dealing with basic problems of our contemporary world. In *The Tao of Physics* Capra writes: "Science does not need mysticism and mysticism does not need science, but man needs both."[25] To be more specific, Capra argues that an intellectual understanding of physical reality must be wedded with a profound religious awareness in order to address current problems such as the deteriorating environment. If we ask what leads to the conviction that there is a parallel between physics and mysticism, the answer seems to lie in the experience of a *single unified whole*. Whereas classical physics in the Newtonian tradition was highly reductionistic and dealt with individual parts of reality, quantum physics tends to think of physical reality as a unified whole that lies beyond conceptual grasp. There are several quantum phenomena that could be mentioned in this regard, but I will limit myself at this point to one of the most dramatic, namely the phenomenon known as "quantum entanglement".

Before I explain some of the technical aspects of the experiments indicating quantum entanglement, I would like to suggest a fictitious analogy that may help intuitively. We have to imagine a time before modern communication when messages from Europe to the United States took a considerable amount of time. We imagine further that there is a married couple living in New York City and another married couple living in Zurich, Switzerland. The New York couple enjoys every morning at 8:00 either a cup of coffee or a cup of tea, but never both on the same day. The Zurich couple enjoys every afternoon at 2:00 either a cup of coffee or a cup of tea, but never both on the same day. Now we keep a log of the events on both sides of the Atlantic—whether the New York couple has coffee or tea and whether the Zurich couple has coffee or tea—and what we discover is astonishing. Without exception, when the New York couple has coffee, the Zurich couple has tea. And when the New York couple has tea, the Zurich couple has coffee. Note: The events are taking place at the same time, given the six-hour time difference, and there is no possibility of communication between the two. Therefore, a causal connection between the two events is excluded, but nevertheless, the events are perfectly correlated. This analogy gives us an intuitive understanding of what is happening on the quantum level of reality.

I will not go into great detail about the experiments indicating the correlation of quantum events, and I beg the indulgence of those who have studied quantum physics and find my presentation an oversimplification. Let us consider a laboratory apparatus that generates two electrons whose total spin angular momentum is zero. This means that one of the electrons spins clockwise, and the other spins counterclockwise. We will generate these two particles so that they are propelled in opposite directions, and we will set detectors on both sides to measure the spin of the two electrons. On our first trial, we shoot the electrons toward the detectors and discover that one of them has a clockwise spin, the other a counterclockwise spin. Now in front of one detector, we place a magnetic device that can change the spin direction of an electron before it hits the detector. With this arrangement, we should expect to find that both electrons have the same spin. If the electron traveling to the left has a clockwise and the one traveling to the right has a counter-clockwise spin and if we change the one traveling left from clockwise to counterclockwise, our detectors should measure the same spin for both electrons. What we discover on our second trial is, however, quite surprising. When we change the spin direction of the electron traveling to the left, the spin direction of the one traveling to the right is also changed! How did this happen? Well, perhaps the electron on the left sent a message to the one on the right, and this message caused a change of spin direction.

Since it is generally assumed that messages cannot be sent at speeds faster than light, we want to exclude the possibility of message-sending and then record the results again. So we move our detectors to a distance from the electron generator that would render it physically impossible for a light signal from the left electron to reach the right electron after the left one has undergone a spin change. We try the experiment again and find that the spin direction on the right electron changed, just as it had on the second trial. The greater-than-light-speed distance between the two electrons excludes the possibility of causation in our time-space-continuum, but nevertheless the correlation is an undeniable event. This experiment has been performed many times, as a rule using polarized photons instead of electrons, but the correlation of the events is always confirmed. The most common interpretation of this situation is the following. At the quantum level, the idea of location in space no longer has any meaning because nothing is ultimately separable from anything else. Physicists have termed this situation *non-locality* or *non-separability* of quantum reality. Furthermore, this quantum reality is at some level *our* reality. Everything in our immediate physical environment is made up of quanta that have been interacting with other quanta in this manner from the Big Bang down to the present. Whether one wants to speak of a deeper reality or a transcendent reality, there is a reality more fundamental than the one we perceive with the five senses, a reality that is not restricted by time and space and in which non-causal interactions occur because everything is ultimately connected.

It is the awareness of the profound connectivity of the universe, this holistic understanding of the universe, which has led some physicists to search out parallels with the mystical experience of the One. Einstein himself had spoken of the experience of a *single significant whole*, of the deep *rationality of the universe*, and he called this the "cosmic religious feeling". But the holistic experience of the non-causal, non-local quantum world does not seem to be rational in the sense in which Einstein meant it; that is, it doesn't seem to be strictly causal and completely subject to mathematical analysis. Nevertheless, I myself am skeptical of the attempt to identify the holistic experience of the quantum reality—if indeed it can be experienced—with the mystical experience of unity either in its Eastern or Western form. I do, however, see an interesting parallel with the ancient Stoic notion of a "natural law" or "reason". For the Stoics, reason was not understood in a mathematical, but rather in a metaphysical sense as a guiding principle permeating the universe. The sense of a deep rationality in the universe is precisely what Cicero describes in *On the Laws* as the natural basis of justice, law, ethics and religion; he calls it the *lex naturalis* ("natural law").

Taking Cicero as our guide, it would be interesting to explore the political and moral implications of non-separability as it is understood in quantum physics. This approach would have the advantage of being independent of any organized religion and could possibly lead to results acceptable to human beings as human beings. Of these implications, one of the more fundamental would certainly be the following: Corresponding to the entanglement of particles on the quantum level is the *moral complicity of individuals* on the human level. In a world where everything is connected, and each thing interacts with everything else, we can no longer think in atomistic terms of individuals as independent and self-sufficient beings. We can no longer make black-and-white distinctions between some people who are good and others who are bad, some who are innocent and others who are guilty. We are all connected, and we are all somehow complicit in whatever happens, admittedly to a greater or lesser extent. When a heinous crime is committed, somebody has to go to prison; it's not possible to imprison everyone who is remotely complicit. But we could recognize this complicity and take the necessary steps to improve the situation in which the crime occurred.

On a political level, the holistic view of the quantum entanglement would suggest *the primacy of the common good over individual rights*. The modern notion of human rights developed during the Enlightenment period of eighteenth-century Europe, where it received considerable impetus from the atomistic understanding of reality; just as each atom has its own properties, each individual has certain inalienable rights. Unlike human rights, the idea of the common good developed in Stoicism, where the phrase *bonum commune* ("common good") is first attested in the writings of Seneca. Admittedly, the notion of the common good is difficult to define, and even if we arrive at a plausible definition, it is difficult to keep the common good in mind when there is such a strong emphasis in our society on individual human rights. Nevertheless, we should at least try to view human rights and the common good as complementary approaches to social and political problems.

In summary, the non-separability of quantum events and the holistic view of reality that they imply have their counterparts in the moral complicity of the individual and in the responsibility of all citizens for the common good. Furthermore, I am suggesting that this insight should be considered against the background of natural law in the Stoic tradition. Thereby, I am not advocating a return to Stoic philosophy, but rather a reevaluation of natural law in view of our contemporary understanding of the physical universe.

Without claiming completeness, I offer the following closing reflections on our topic:

1) The analysis of personal or political situations always requires an *abstraction from the whole,* and since this abstraction can be performed in various ways, multiple constellations are possible. For instance, when we discuss the relations between Iran and the United States, do we abstract a timeline beginning in 1979 or in 1953? The decision about this will have a considerable impact on the interpretation of events. Although such abstraction is unavoidable, it is crucial that participants in dialogue bear in mind that the constellation of events under discussion is not the only possible abstraction, since history as well as the universe is characterized by connectivity.

2) There are *no absolutes* in human relationships, whereby one could argue that some individuals are innocent, whereas others are guilty. In individual and historical conflicts, the boundaries between good and bad, right and wrong are always blurred. Ordinary domestic disputes build a class of interactions in which it is generally recognized that neither party is completely without fault. The same should be recognized in the political realm.

3) *Defensible moral judgments* are only possible when the individuals passing judgment recognize and take into account their own complicity in the events under consideration. Failure to recognize this complicity is a clear indication that too much of the whole has been eliminated through abstraction, thus rendering sound judgment impossible.

4) *Retribution for wrongdoing* requires not only the punishment of overt culprits, but also significant behavioral and policy modifications by all complicit parties. A prime example of moral complicity is the complacency of the middle class with regard to the social, political and economic conditions that produce poverty and thus exacerbate criminal behavior.

5) The notion of *human rights* should be interpreted in the context of moral complicity and responsibility for the common good. Human rights tend to be atomistic, i.e. rights of the individual as such, whereas moral complicity and the primacy of the common good are based on the fundamental and necessary interrelatedness of human beings.

7

Human Rights Revisited

"Life, liberty and the pursuit of happiness"—this is without doubt one of the best-known phrases in American history. It is probably safe to assume that almost every American knows the phrase, although many may not be sure whether it appears in the Declaration of Independence, in the body of the Constitution or in the Amendments to the Constitution, that is, the Bill of Rights. As I am sure all of *you* know, it occurs in the Declaration of Independence, which was authored to some great extent by Thomas Jefferson. Herein we read:

> We hold these truths to be self-evident, that all men are created equal, that they are endowed by their Creator with certain unalienable Rights, that among these are Life, Liberty and the pursuit of Happiness.—That to secure these rights, Governments are instituted among Men, deriving their just powers from the consent of the governed,—That whenever any Form of Government becomes destructive of these ends, it is the Right of the People to alter or to abolish it, and to institute new Government, laying its foundation on such principles and organizing its powers in such form, as to them shall seem most likely to effect their Safety and Happiness.

In reading this historic statement, there are two ideas that stand out clearly. Firstly, these inalienable rights—life, liberty and the pursuit of happiness—are essentially the possession of the *individual* and only indirectly apply to the *group*. Only because every individual has these rights can we say that a group of people have them; human rights apply essentially to the individual. Secondly, these rights provide sufficient and legitimate reason for *action*. If these rights are being denied, the individual has the additional right to respond in whatever way necessary in order to ensure that these rights are respected. As we shall see, these two characteristics of human rights, namely that they apply to individuals and that they legitimize action, can lead under certain circumstances to apparently unresolvable contradictions. When the rights of Mr Smith conflict with the rights of Ms Jones, the matter of human rights ceases to be simply a moral issue and becomes very often a legal dispute. Or to take a more specific case: When the rights of the unborn baby conflict with the rights of the expectant mother, how do we pass moral judgment? Given the central role of the concept of human rights in contemporary moral and legal thought, it seems to me that it is worth investigating the origin of the notion. When did the notion of a "human right" first appear and in what context? Furthermore, what were the factors that contributed to its development into an international concept?

Returning to the Declaration of Independence, it is interesting to note the following. The statement in the Declaration of Independence about life, liberty and the pursuit of happiness is very similar to a statement written about one hundred years earlier in England by John Locke. In his *Two Treatises of Government*, published in 1690, Locke writes: "The *State of Nature* has a Law of Nature to govern it, which obliges every one: And Reason, which is that Law, teaches all Mankind, who will consult it, that being all equal and independent, no one ought to harm another in his Life, Health, Liberty, or Possessions."[26(2.6)] The mention of "possessions" is particularly interesting because it occurs also in the US Bill of Rights; in Amendment V to the Constitution we read: nor shall any person "be deprived of life, liberty, or property, without due process of law…" The fact that *property* is mentioned in the Bill of Rights instead of the *pursuit of happiness* may indicate more clearly a conscious reliance on the philosophy of John Locke. In any case, we can establish without doubt that the idea of human rights did not originate in the United States; its roots go back at least to seventeenth-century England. Since then, the concept has not only been adopted in the US, but it has also attained international recognition. Following the atrocities of the Second World War, the General Assembly of the United Nations adopted on 10 December 1948 the Universal Declaration of Human Rights. Yet, the question remains: What was the origin of the concept of human rights?

It is well known that the Greek philosophers, notably Plato and Aristotle, were intensely interested in the concept of "justice" or "right"; they did not, however, develop the concept of "human rights" in the modern sense. If we look for the historical roots of the idea of human rights, we will discover that the notion grew out of Hellenistic philosophy of the third century BC, specifically out of the philosophy of the Stoics. Nevertheless, the differences between the Stoic idea of "right" and our idea of "rights" are striking. According to the Stoics, the entire cosmos is permeated by an eternal moral law that guarantees justice. The Stoics spoke about the natural law (*lex naturalis*) or natural right (*ius naturale*) that guided the actions of human beings, and those individuals who lived in accordance with natural right were said to be virtuous, that is, morally good. One of our best sources for Stoic philosophy is Cicero, and in his writing entitled *On the Laws* (*De legibus*), he has an extended section on natural law or natural right. Before any law was written and before any state was constituted, there was the highest law of the universe, a force of nature (*vis naturae*), which commands that certain things be done and prohibits that other things be done. This law is the highest reason; it is rooted in nature; and it is perfected in the minds of human beings. It is precisely this eternal law that distinguishes between right and wrong, between justice and injustice.[27(1.18f)] Although the highest law is everywhere to be found in nature, human beings have a privileged position in the search for it because this eternal law is identical with right reason. Following the dictates of right reason is obedience to the law of natural right.

Cicero notes further that right reason or the law of natural right in the universe binds all human beings together so that the entire universe can be considered as a common state (*civitas*). We as human beings are born with a sense of natural right and wrong, and therefore to be truly human, we must exercise justice in relating to each other. We are prone by nature to love our fellow human beings,[27(1.34f)] and anyone who denies justice to another person destroys something within himself.[28(3.33)] That is, the punishment for non-compliance with natural right is self-estrangement. In summary, the Stoic idea of natural right was *cosmic*, rather than *individual*. To be sure, natural right motivated a person to action—not, however, in the sense of insisting on one's own rights, but rather in the sense of obligating one to act in a certain way. Natural right was not a *claimed* right, but rather an *obligating* right. It was not a purely subjective possession of the individual, but rather an objective order of the universe governing the individual's conduct.

Those of you who are familiar with the Christian tradition may recognize some of these thoughts from the writings of the Apostle Paul. In his letter to the church at Rome, Paul utilizes some of the Stoic ideas about natural right in order to demonstrate that human beings as such understand the moral demands of the law. He writes: "When Gentiles who have not the law do by nature what the law requires, they are a law to themselves, even though they do not have the law. They show that what the law requires is written on their hearts..." (Romans 2.14–15). Mediated through Paul, the notion of an eternal, unwritten law, that is, the concept of natural right, became a part of Christian thought from the Patristic period of the second century through the classic formulation of Catholic theology in the works of St Thomas Aquinas in the thirteenth century. Although the notion of natural right was integrated into Christian theology, none of these theologians developed the concept of human rights in the modern sense. To put it more bluntly, the concept of human rights is not, in my opinion, an essentially Christian idea. Certainly, it occurs nowhere in the Christian Bible nor is it to be found in early Christian literature. There is at present no consensus among historians about the exact origin of the modern concept of human rights, but I do not see it emerging before the late Renaissance period. With a moment's reflection, the reason for this should be sufficiently clear. The Roman Catholic Church emphasized the idea of community so strongly that the situation in Europe was not conducive to the development of individual claim-rights. The concept of a natural right remained an *obligation* to obedience, not a *claim* for benefits.

The transition from an understanding of natural right as an objective, governing principle to an understanding of human rights as a subjective claim on others took place over several centuries, but the most significant changes occurred in the seventeenth century. I mentioned earlier that John Locke wrote about life and liberty a century before the Declaration of Independence. When we read the entire section in his *Two Treatises of Government*, we discover, perhaps to our surprise, that he was not talking about claim-rights, but rather about duties. He writes: "The *State of Nature* has a Law of Nature to govern it, which obliges every one: And Reason, which is that Law, teaches all Mankind, who will consult it, that being all equal and independent, no one ought to harm another in his Life, Health, Liberty, or Possessions."[26(2.6)] These are clearly Stoic ideas, which Locke took over from the philosophical tradition.

In the writings of Thomas Hobbes, on the other hand, the modern concept of human rights begins to emerge clearly: a natural right understood as a *claim*, not as a *duty*. Equally clear is that this transition took place under the influence of the emerging classical physics of the seventeenth century. What was groundbreaking in the political philosophy of Thomas Hobbes was his application of Galileo's investigation of the motion of bodies and his atomistic view of matter to an understanding of the commonwealth. Hobbes assumed that in the original state of nature human beings were like atoms; each one had certain innate rights, but they were not bound together in a community. That is to say, the individual, not the community, was for Hobbes the fundamental fact of nature, and the right of nature was something that the individual possessed, not something that governed the conduct of society. In his *Leviathan* (1651), Hobbes writes:

> The RIGHT OF NATURE, which Writers commonly call *Jus Naturale*, is the Liberty each man hath, to use his own power, as he will himselfe, for the preservation of his own Nature; that is to say, of his own Life; and consequently, of doing any thing, which in his own Judgment, and Reason, hee shall conceive to be the aptest means thereunto.[29]

According to Hobbes, the state of nature is one in which every individual has a right to everything he deems necessary for survival. Since there are no restrictions on this fundamental right of nature, the state of nature turns out to be one of constant war. Everyone has a right to everything, and the conflicting rights lead necessarily to perpetual war. In order to attain a peaceful coexistence in a state, all individuals must agree contractually to give up the right of nature to everything. Hobbes' right of nature is clearly a *claim-right*, not a *duty-right*. My right to preserve my own life gives me the right to claim whatever means are necessary to that end. In this context, the obligation of natural right in Cicero's sense loses its meaning.

Galileo died in 1642, and in the same year, Sir Isaac Newton was born. In many ways, Newton brought the work of scientists like Kepler and Galileo to a conclusion. He developed a comprehensive understanding of the motion of bodies and elaborated on the atomistic view of matter. Looking back on the seventeenth century, we can say: *What Sir Isaac Newton accomplished in physics, Thomas Hobbes accomplished in political theory.* Newton rejected the medieval, Aristotelian conception of the world; he adopted the Epicurean understanding that the world is composed of atoms; and he developed an atomistic, mechanistic worldview. In the second edition of his *Opticks*, Newton writes:

> All these things being considered, it seems probable to me, that God in the beginning formed matter in solid, massy, hard, impenetrable, moveable particles; of such sizes and figures, and with such other properties, and in such proportion to space, as most conduced to the end for which he formed them; and that these primitive particles being solids, are incomparably harder than any Porous bodies compounded of them; even so very hard, as never to wear or break in pieces: no ordinary power being able to divide what God himself made One, in the first creation.[23(p260)]

Hobbes proceeded along similar lines in his political philosophy. He adopted the Epicurean concept of atoms and viewed society as if it were a collection of atoms. For Hobbes, the fundamental building block of society is the individual with his right of nature to self-preservation.

The political philosophy of Thomas Hobbes has had a tremendous impact on Western societies. The understanding of the individual as the building block of society and the concomitant emphasis on individual rights are the roots of many contemporary moral and political points of view. That the emphasis on the individual and his or her rights can lead to unresolvable conflicts, I have already mentioned with regard to the debate over abortion. On an international level, we have an apparently unresolvable debate between two groups of people in the Middle East, one claiming the right of self-defense and security, the other claiming the right of self-determination and freedom. Within the context of human rights, both claims seem to be legitimate, and yet the claims taken together lead us into an impasse. What we need in my opinion is an additional perspective that supplements the notion of human rights. Not only is the concept of human rights problematic in actual practice, but the advancement of theoretical physics in the twentieth century has made it abundantly clear that the atomistic, mechanistic view of the world that underpinned individual rights is untenable. Atoms are not the ultimate building blocks of the world; there is a connectivity of the universe that mandates a return to a more holistic view of society, specifically to the notion of the common good.

A discussion of the specific scientific developments that altered the context of our thinking lies beyond the scope of the present essay, but for those of you who are interested in physics, I simply mention that I am alluding to the phenomenon of quantum entanglement and non-locality. Having said that, I would like to present once again the analogy that I utilized in a previous essay ("Physics, Religion and Natural Law") in order to approach the phenomenon intuitively. Let us imagine a time before modern communication when messages from Europe to the United States took a considerable amount of time. We imagine further that there is a married couple living in New York City and another married couple living in Zurich, Switzerland. The New York couple enjoys every morning at 8:00 either a cup of coffee or a cup of tea, but never both on the same day. The Zurich couple enjoys every afternoon at 2:00 either a cup of coffee or a cup of tea, but never both on the same day. Now we keep a log of the events on both sides of the Atlantic—whether the New York couple has coffee or tea and whether the Zurich couple has coffee or tea—and what we discover is astonishing. Without exception, when the New York couple has coffee, the Zurich couple has tea. And when the New York couple has tea, the

Zurich couple has coffee. Since there is a six-hour time difference between New York and Zurich, the correlated events are taking place at the same time, and therefore, there is no possibility of communication between the two. A causal connection is excluded, but nevertheless, the events are perfectly correlated. This analogy gives us an intuitive understanding of what is happening on the quantum level of reality.

At the quantum level, the idea of location in space no longer has any meaning because nothing is ultimately separable from anything else. Physicists have termed this situation non-locality or non-separability of quantum reality. Considering that everything in our immediate physical environment is made up of quanta that have been interacting with other quanta since the Big Bang, the quantum reality of non-separability must be understood as fundamental to *our* reality. Whether one wants to speak of a deeper reality or a transcendent reality, the fact is inescapable: There is a reality more fundamental than the one we perceive with the five senses—a reality that is not restricted by time and space and in which non-causal interactions occur because everything is ultimately connected.

Such revolutionary discoveries in quantum physics have placed Newtonian physics in a new light. Was the classical physics of Newton wrong? The answer to this question is: yes and no. On the level of everyday experience, the basic principles that we learn in an introductory physics course are totally adequate. If we are calculating the velocity of a falling object or if we are building a bridge, the laws of classical physics are applicable. If, however, we are dealing with a situation on the subatomic level, the classical laws are no longer accurate. Likewise, when we ask the question whether the concept of human rights is wrong, the answer must be: yes and no. In many situations, the notion of human rights is very useful and can lead to morally responsible results. But human rights must always be seen against the background of natural right, and in some situations, it is only this natural right in the form of the common good that can lead us out of the impasse of conflicting rights.

By emphasizing natural right, I am not advocating a return to Stoic philosophy or to the political thought of Cicero. The pre-scientific idea of a timeless moral law or an unchanging natural right in the universe is in the twenty-first century no longer tenable. Rather, I am maintaining that some modern form of natural right is necessary as a counterbalance to the concept of human rights. Clearly, this natural right need not be timeless and unchanging, although it must be relatively stable in a particular culture and in a particular historical period. Furthermore, the delineation of such a natural right must take into account an understanding of nature in general as well as human nature in particular. Only in this way can the notion of the common good be protected from the fascist abuse that sets the good of the nation above the good of the people comprising the nation. Placing human rights in the context of the natural right and the common good may not be totally adequate for our time, but it is at least a beginning.

8

Individual Interests and the Common Good

I have chosen as a topic for this essay "Individual Interests and the Common Good", and I am proposing for consideration the thesis that societies are partially and in some cases predominately defined by the relationship between the interests of the individual and concern for the common good. Grasping the relationship between individual interests and the common good involves, on the one hand, an understanding of both concepts. Which individual interests are considered legitimate in the society? And how is the common good to be understood? On the other hand, the relationship between the two involves a balance, whereby either individual interests or the common good may be given more weight. At the risk of oversimplification, I suggest that individual interests and the common good have come to be understood in American society in the following way. The supreme individual interest is individual *freedom*, understood in a libertarian sense, and the defining common good is *security*, understood as national security, which protects all Americans from foreign aggression.

That security as a common good could be understood differently should be apparent. One could, for instance, think of financial security as a common good. That would mean that every American had a minimum income that would provide for an acceptable standard of health and happiness. Or, one could understand the defining common good as education since an educated public is a necessary condition of a functioning democracy. Similarly, it should be obvious that individual freedom could be conceived other than in libertarian terms. To be sure, the notion of individual freedom may always be correlated in some way with human rights, but characteristic of libertarianism is the focus of human rights on property ownership, where "property" is understood either as a *person* or as *inanimate objects*. In both cases, full ownership is asserted; just as an individual can have full ownership of material property, so also the individual has full ownership of himself. From a libertarian point of view, justice obtains in a society when the rights of individuals to their persons and to their possessions have been respected. Oddly enough, libertarian tendencies join the "right wing" of American society with the "left wing". On economic matters, the right wing is libertarian and emphasizes its right to property, including natural resources. On social matters, the left wing is libertarian, stressing the right of the individual to make decisions about his or her own body (abortion and sex transformation, for instance). Both parties agree that the State should not interfere with their individual freedoms, but rather should protect their human rights by enacting the necessary laws. It is certainly possible, however, to correlate the notion of individual freedom with human rights without espousing a libertarian moral and political philosophy. If we eliminate the focus on property ownership and the control of property, individual freedom could still include the right of free speech, the right of due process and so forth. We could continue this analysis on the variations of individual interests and the common good, but enough has been said to indicate that some underlying, guiding principle must be at work in defining these terms and arriving at a balance between them.

In another context, I have discussed at some length the corporatization of American and European societies and have identified the transfer of Darwinian thinking to the social, political and economic spheres as one of the most characteristic elements of this process. Not only has corporate America adopted a crude form of Darwinism to justify its unfeeling and brutal tactics in the business world, but it has also promoted the transfer of this model to the social sphere. As soon as the whole of society is understood to operate on a Darwinian model, we arrive at a type of social Darwinism that becomes the underlying principle for defining legitimate individual interests and a plausible common good. In the societal arena, the fight for survival becomes a fight for dominance, and the end always justifies whatever means must be employed. Furthermore, the common good is no longer related to the welfare of individuals, but rather to an abstract concept such as the survival of the species or the security of the nation.

It is well known that Darwin himself was skeptical about this transfer of a biological model to the social realm, but it is seldom recognized that this type of social Darwinism was a defining element in the fascist societies of the Second World War. Much of the brutality of the Nazis was philosophically justified through the writings of Ernst Haeckel who introduced social Darwinism to the German intelligentsia. During the period of National Socialism in Germany, the common good was understood to be the welfare of the nation, and to this end, the rights of individuals were abused and the lives of individuals were sacrificed. In 1933, Paul von Hindenburg and Adolf Hitler declared that Germany was in a state of emergency and that in order to protect the German people and the German nation, it was necessary to restrict the rights of individuals in certain ways. In the famous "Decree of the Reich President for the Protection of the People and the State", they nullified basic constitutional rights of the individual such as freedom of speech, freedom of assembly, freedom of the press, privacy of postal and telegraph communications, and protection from house searches. On a personal note: My doctoral adviser in Zurich, Switzerland was born in Berlin-Steglitz, was a student in Germany during the Third Reich and remembered well how the Nazis made an unwarranted search of his room, looking for books that were on the list of forbidden reading material. In fascist societies, the welfare of the individual is sacrificed for the common good, whereby the common good is now understood abstractly as national security.

The development of social Darwinism in the United States took a different path, one of the key figures being the British philosopher and sociologist Herbert Spencer. Whether Spencer was a true Darwinist and a strict libertarian is a question of dispute, but it is indisputable that he was interpreted in this way by industrialists such as Andrew Carnegie. Furthermore, this interpretation does find some support in the writings of Spencer. As Darwin himself acknowledged, it was Spencer who coined the phrase "survival of the fittest", and in his well-known work *The Man versus the State* (1884), Spencer characterized the poor as the "good-for-nothings" of society, whose suffering is the just reward for their inability and misconduct.[30(p113f)] In accordance with the principles of libertarianism, he considered justice to be equivalent to individual freedom, and individual freedom meant for him the absence of forcible interference from other persons and from the state. The reception of Spencer's thought in America led to the growth of a type of *libertarian Darwinism*, which has had a tremendous impact on our culture. In the context of libertarian Darwinism, the "common good" can be understood either in an abstract sense as in the case of national security or in a restricted concrete sense, whereby the so-called "common" good applies only to a particular group of individuals. Whether the group in question is right-wing or left-wing is irrelevant from the standpoint of the *common* good; then, the good that is sought in both cases benefits only a small group.

The problem of individual interests and the common good has a long history, dating back at least as far as the Greek city-states. It concerned both Plato and Aristotle in their political philosophies, although they did not speak expressly of the common *good*. In his work *On Laws*, Plato spoke of that which was a *common benefit* to all citizens in the city-state, and Aristotle followed him later in using this phrase. According to Plato, the city-state must be founded on the notion of common benefit, which means that there must be a certain equality among the citizens. This equality is not, however, a monetary one; Plato never envisioned a form of communism in which a financial equality was established and private ownership was abolished. The equality of the citizens, who in many ways were unequal, lay in the justice afforded to each. Society is not established in order to benefit an elite few, but rather to guarantee justice to all. The assumption of Plato was that the individual interests of the citizens would be best served if the common benefit of justice to all was attained. The underlying guiding principle of this balance between individual interests and the common good was an understanding of the universe as founded on the highest principles of goodness and as governed by a type of divine law. Plato's model for thinking about the common good was not the competitive jungle of social Darwinism where the strongest survive and the weakest are considered disposable, but rather the harmony of a well-functioning organism in which every individual plays an indispensable role and every individual benefits. In contrast to political philosophers such as Thomas Hobbes, Plato did not think of society as an aggregate of individual units. If it were, one might conclude that the best possible common good had been attained when the majority of citizens had benefited. Such a view, however, Plato could not accept. In his mind, society is an organism whose well-being depends on the proper functioning of each part. The whole cannot be happy if some of its parts are suffering.

In his work *The Republic*, Plato compares the *civic* life to the *psychic* and draws some very interesting parallels. If the parts of the psyche are in conflict with each other, the entire psychic life of the individual is an unhappy one. Allowing free rein to the sensual impulses of the psyche produces a disharmony with the individual's awareness of higher values; passion comes into conflict with reason. Passions of the psyche are not in principle bad, but they need the direction of reason so that they do not disrupt the overall harmony. According to Plato, we find peace of mind only when a harmony between passion and reason is attained. Given this framework, personal justice consists in a harmony in the psyche, whereby each part of the psyche performs the function assigned to it by nature. Similarly, civic justice consists in a harmony in society, whereby each member performs the duties for which he is by nature suited. The common good is not simply something that each member *receives*; the common good is something that each member *performs*. Plato envisions a society in which each member according to his natural abilities and talents makes a contribution to society as a whole.[31] He is concerned about a certain pattern of interaction among the citizens of the society. In a just society where the common good is promoted, every citizen should enjoy a measure of prosperity and happiness and should contribute to the prosperity and happiness of others. Finally, the structural similarity between the psychic life and the civic life is rooted in a transcendent, eternal pattern. The harmony of the psyche and that of the city-state reflect the harmony of the transcendent realm of ideas. There is in Plato's mind a transcendent moral order to which the individual and society as a whole are to conform. It is at this point that Plato touches on the notion of *natural law*, which was later developed fully by the Stoics and which finds expression in Cicero's *On the Laws* and *On the Commonwealth*.

In conclusion, we should note that in Plato's view individual interests do not provide a viable basis for society; individual interests tend to separate citizens, whereas the common benefit or common good join them together. Secondly, the common good in society is justice, i.e. an organized pattern of interaction among the citizens that benefits everyone. Thirdly, Plato's understanding of society is based on the model of an organism in which each citizen makes a contribution to the commonwealth. Fourthly, in promoting justice or the common good, society emulates an eternal pattern; that is, Plato's view is based on the conviction that there is a transcendent moral order. If we remove this transcendent moral order, if we lose sight of a divine law permeating the universe, if we no longer perceive the eternal *in* time, then Plato's understanding of a just society working for the common good collapses. In a fully secular world or, to be more explicit, in an atheistic world such as ours, it is difficult to find any reason to work for the common good, and since the idea of justice is no longer rooted in the eternal, it can easily be understood in a libertarian sense.

The modern reader will identify numerous problems with the thoughts of Plato, not the least of which will be the idea of an unchanging moral order, but for the present, I would like to concentrate on just one aspect, namely the parallel between the psyche and the city-state. Just as the passions of the psyche are to be held in check by the faculty of reason, so also the workers of the city-state are to be under the guidance of the counselors. That is, by reproducing the hierarchical structure of the psyche in society, some members of society are necessarily under the control and guidance of others. The "intelligent few" must be in control so that society functions properly. Obviously, a democracy cannot function in this way, but it is well known that Plato rejected the concept of democracy as a viable form of government. Perhaps, he himself was aware of the dangers lurking in his political theory and hoped that the common good would be served if he designated a wise philosopher as the king. Unfortunately, he seems to have underestimated the extent to which power corrupts, and as we know, the idea that a wise leader would preserve the common good for the whole of society has proven historically to be an illusion.

If we are to learn from Plato, we must modify his understanding of the common good in two essential ways. First of all, although it was a significant insight of Plato to correlate the life of the psyche with the civic life, his understanding of the psyche contained two very problematic aspects: its structure was hierarchical, and it presupposed an unchanging pattern. If we eliminate these two elements, we could search plausibly for parallels between human existence and human society that might prove very enlightening. Secondly, the possibility of the *common* good mutating into a good for the *few* suggests that individual human rights are a necessary complement to the common good in order to ensure the well-being of all individuals.

In the final section of this essay, I will sketch out briefly my understanding of the common good and individual interests, taking as a guiding principle not the "survival of the fittest" from the organic realm, but rather the "connectivity of all things" from the area of quantum physics. The ultimate reality of the universe is not *competition*, but rather *correlation* or *correspondence*. One event calls forth another; the second corresponds to the first; and so the universe advances, weaving together a pattern of correlations. In the realm of human existence, this is not a Marxist dialectic that requires resistance, struggle and revolution. It is a true co-responding, based on dialogue, diplomacy and mutual benefit. The connectivity of all things means that we do not live just for ourselves and that the libertarian notion of full self-ownership is an illusion. As both Plato and Cicero stressed, we live to a great extent for those around us, for family and friends, and for the society in which we find ourselves. The words of Cicero are an impressive testimony:

We are not born for ourselves alone, to use Plato's splendid words, but our country claims for itself one part of our birth, and our friends another. Moreover, as the Stoics believe, everything produced on the earth is created for the use of mankind, and *men are born for the sake of men, so that they may be able to assist one another*. Consequently, we ought in this to follow nature as our leader, to contribute to the community "common benefits" (*communes utilitates*), and, by the exchange of dutiful services, by giving and receiving expertise and effort and means, to bind fast the fellowship of men with each other.[32](1.22)

As human beings, we were born to assist each other and to work for the common good. Any group, whether it be conservative or liberal, that insists on certain human rights from a libertarian perspective of self-ownership has lost sight of what it means to be human. To be truly *human* rights, these rights cannot be separated from the human condition which is defined at its deepest level by mutual connectivity. In other words, human rights outside the context of the common good cease to quality as *human* rights.

Although the common good has both a personal and a societal dimension, I am for the present only concerned about the societal dimension. There are certain fundamental processes in society that seem to be determinative for the well-being of individuals; among these processes are the attaining of self-knowledge, the developing of the self and the transforming of relationships. It may seem odd at first to consider self-knowledge and self-development as societal processes, but there are in fact numerous institutions that are clustered around self-knowledge and self-development, thus lending them a societal dimension. From religious institutions to the publishing industry, we find a dynamic in society promoting self-knowledge and self-development. The transforming of relation-ships is more obviously a societal process and can range from the establishment of friendships in a club to political revolutions. Translated into terms of the common good, these three processes become *peace, opportuneness* and *justice*. I will limit myself to comments on opportuneness because it is the element of the common good that is more clearly temporal in nature. What is opportune is that which fits the present circumstances. "It was an opportune moment", we say. An *opportune* offer of assistance is an offer occurring at an appropriate time. Should the offer be made at some other time, it may be unwelcome or even harmful, given the constellation of factors at that time. An event must be timely or else it does not contribute to the common good. This is an element of the common good that should always be considered when we appeal to human rights. Human rights tend to be understood as relatively permanent. If individuals have human right "A" today, they have it tomorrow and next year as well. The question of the common good is this: Is it opportune to claim this human right here and now? Naturally, individuals will often disagree about the opportuneness of claiming this or that right, but much would be gained if the question were at least posed and openly discussed.

9

Forms of Atheism

When we speak of "atheism", we are usually thinking about the philosophical position that denies the existence of God. To be sure, there are persons who hold this view and who characterize themselves as "atheists". The phenomenon of atheism is, however, much more widespread in American society than the ordinary usage of the word would indicate. In fact, a careful analysis of American culture against the background of the history of religions suggests that atheism is the prevailing attitude of the population as a whole. In the following essay, I will discuss three forms of atheism, which taken together cover a fairly broad spectrum of the culture. These are: *theoretical atheism, practical atheism* and *religious atheism*. Without anticipating too much of the subsequent discussion, I suggest that these three forms are correlated with the "ultimate" in the following way: *Theoretical atheism denies the ultimate; Practical atheism ignores the ultimate; Religious atheism trivializes the ultimate.* The reasons for the choice of the word "ultimate" instead of "God" will become clearer in the course of the essay. The English word "ultimate" derives from the Latin *ultimus*, which is the superlative of *ulter*, meaning "that which is beyond" or "on the other side". Whatever attributes we may assign to the "ultimate", they must be understood as superlatives so that the ultimate remains something without equal.

Of these three forms, theoretical atheism is by far the most consistent and the most rational. To a greater or lesser extent, the theoretical atheist has considered the arguments for and against the existence of God (the ultimate) and has satisfied himself that the evidence speaks in favor of atheism. The theoretical atheist usually adopts a substitute for religion, this being in many cases some form of humanism. To be sure, it is not the humanism of the Renaissance as exemplified, for instance, in the writings of Erasmus of Rotterdam who was certainly not an atheist. Rather, the theoretical atheist is more likely to appeal to the humanism of the Enlightenment and may find a comrade in Voltaire. Or this person may be more influenced by the development of modern science and thus have more affinity to the Freethinkers of the nineteenth century such as Thomas Huxley. The particular substitution for religion is determined to a great extent by the personality and education of the theoretical atheist. Voltaire would support the theoretical atheist in dealing with the problem of human suffering; his famous poem after the Lisbon earthquake of 1755 brings into sharp focus the problem that human suffering poses for believing in the existence of God. On the other hand, Thomas Huxley, the great defender of Charles Darwin, was of scientific bent and set the evolution of the human species over against the biblical account of creation in such a way that the theoretical atheist will be confirmed in his judgment. The theoretical atheist who turns either to humanism or to freethinking will be very often adamant about social issues and willing to engage in social action in the interest of the underprivileged. Far from being a detriment to society, the theoretical atheist reflects in many cases the highest ethical and moral standards.

The greatest weakness of theoretical atheism lies in its uncritical acceptance of an outdated and often vague notion of the ultimate. Various human experiences such as suffering and scientific theories such as evolution are analyzed in considerable detail in relation to a primitive concept of the ultimate. It is as though one set out to evaluate the validity of the concepts of chemistry by investigating the ideas of the old alchemists. An accurate evaluation of the atheistic position requires that we take into account understandings of the ultimate on the same intellectual plane as the scientific theories that we are considering.

The debate between Paul Tillich and Albert Einstein illustrates the point well.

In September 1940, Union Theological Seminary hosted the "Conference on Science, Philosophy and Religion" and invited Albert Einstein to participate. Einstein held a talk entitled "Science and Religion", in which he rejected the idea of a personal God because it contradicts the scientific understanding of nature.[24(p44–49)] Following the conference, Paul Tillich responded in an article entitled "The Idea of the Personal God", in which he agrees with Einstein that the idea of a personal God would be a contradiction of scientific theory *if* we are assuming a very primitive idea of God, but it is precisely at this point that Tillich launches his criticism of Einstein's ideas about religion. According to Tillich, Einstein's entire argument presupposed a primitive notion of God that no contemporary theologian still holds. He writes: "I want to ask Einstein and every critic of theology to deal with theology in the same fairness which is demanded from everyone who deals, for instance, with physics—namely to attack the most advanced and not some obsolete forms of a discipline."[33(p9)] Tillich himself understood the idea of the personal God as a symbol for a reality that could not be grasped in ordinary language. The criticism that Tillich directed toward Einstein is still relevant today for anyone who wants to criticize intellectually Christian theology. The idea that religious faith requires a "sacrifice of the intellect" (the so-called *sacrificium intellectus*) and, therefore, a rejection of certain scientific theories may still be propagated widely by Christian fundamentalists, but it certainly does not represent the view of the most capable theologians of the last hundred years. If the theoretical atheist does not engage the most advanced form of religious thought, then he himself cannot be taken seriously as an intellectual.

Practical atheists do not deny outright the existence of God (the

Citizens of the Broken Compass

ultimate), and when asked, they may well respond by saying that they are simply agnostic. "There could possibly be a higher power out there, but I'm not certain about it", is a common response. Yet, it is not the agnosticism that really characterizes the practical atheist, but rather his disconcerting indifference to the whole matter. The practical atheist simply chooses to ignore the ultimate and sees, therefore, no reason to be concerned about the matter from a theoretical standpoint. In contrast to the theoretical atheist, the practical atheist will not seek out a substitute for religion. Since he doesn't deny outright the value of religion, there is no perceived need for a replacement. Instead, the practical atheist will adopt implicitly a hedonistic attitude and attempt to maximize his pleasure and minimize any inconvenience. Having pushed the ultimate to the edge of human existence, time becomes the domain in which life is to unfold and to be enjoyed as much as possible. The practical atheist will be much less concerned about social issues than the theoretical atheist and much more concerned about the next opportunity for entertainment or the next acquisition of property. The meaning that the theoretical atheist finds in humanism or in freethinking is absent in the life of the practical atheist, and therefore this person is driven to fill every moment of time with something pleasurable—what we commonly call "fun".

The lack of meaning in the life of the practical atheist can become painfully apparent in a crisis situation. Writing about his experiences at Walden, Henry David Thoreau observed that "the mass of men lead lives of quiet desperation". This statement is as valid today as it was in the nineteenth century. What distinguishes our century from that of Thoreau is the extent to which the desperation is concealed through a process of constant distraction, which often occurs in the form of entertainment. In crisis situations such as the death of a family member, a serious financial setback, a divorce or a period of severe depression, the desperation of the practical atheist can lead him back to some

104

traditional form of religion. When the medical profession pronounces the condition of the practical atheist to be terminal, he may suddenly turn to prayer—sometimes to the surprise of family and friends. Since the practical atheist is an agnostic on the theoretical level, a sudden turn to the ultimate remains an open possibility. Whether this turn is a true "conversion" in the sense of William James in his classic work on the psychology of religion, *The Varieties of Religious Experience* (1902), or whether it is simply a final expression of desperation, as it were a "last-ditch effort" before total resignation, cannot be ascertained in advance. Nevertheless, both possibilities are open to the practical atheist, and both possibilities have been documented from the lives of individuals in crisis.

Practical atheists make up a very large segment of our population, and they have made possible the unprecedented growth of the entertainment industry. In her article "Society and Culture" (1960), Hannah Arendt analyzes the fundamental differences between *entertainment* and *culture*. Whereas culture is something to be cultivated and preserved, entertainment is to be consumed. She writes: "Mass society…wants not culture, but entertainment, and the wares offered by the entertainment industry are indeed consumed by society just as are any other consumer goods."[34(p281)] And further: "If we understand by culture what it originally meant (the Roman *cultura*—derived from *colere*, to take care of and preserve and cultivate) then we can say without any exaggeration that a society obsessed with consumption cannot at the same time be cultured or produce a culture."[34(p286)] Many readers will find the words of Arendt harsh, but the distinction she draws between entertainment and culture is an extremely important one and deserves serious consideration. She does not deny that entertainment has an appropriate role to play in our lives, but she criticizes modern societies that allow entertainment to replace culture. Unlike culture, entertainment is ephemeral; it has no permanence; it is here today and gone tomorrow. Whereas culture is the path to self-enrichment and community-building, entertainment is basically a form of distraction from the desperation of which Thoreau wrote and which has become increasingly destructive of personal relationships.

The primary "social" unit of the practical atheist is slowly becoming the "person–flatscreen" relationship, whereby the flat screen can be a television screen, a computer screen or a mobile telephone screen. The emergence of this new "social" unit has been a boon for the entertainment industry, but it has augmented the isolation of the practical atheist and has modified his thought patterns. The television flat screen in particular is a medium of entertainment; whether the latest Hollywood film, the nightly news broadcast or a PBS special is presented, the person in the "person–flatscreen" relationship assumes that there will be a good measure of amusement and pleasure in it. In contrast to personal conversation between two individuals which can promote conceptual thinking, objectivity and problem-solving, the "person–flatscreen" relationship depends on entertainment for its very existence.

Even more surprising than the presence of the theoretical atheist and the practical atheist in contemporary society is the third form: the religious atheist. The religious atheist shares many characteristics with the practical atheist, but this person is distinguished from the latter by his active engagement in religious practices and/or in a religious community. The common element between the two is the dominance of entertainment. Religion turned into entertainment is the hallmark of religious atheism. The religious atheist does not deny the existence of God, nor does he ignore ostensibly the ultimate in daily life. Instead, the religious atheist trivializes the ultimate to the point that it is no longer *ultimate*. Bumper stickers and meaningless slogans replace serious dialogue and an earnest search for truth. Churches become entertainment centers competing with the music and film industry, and church members are treated as customers who need to be satisfied. The trivializing of the ultimate, which occurs in slogans such as "Keep God in America", allows for the conflation of religion and patriotism so that the Apostles' Creed and the Pledge of Alliance easily merge together in the mind of the religious atheist. Since the ultimate is no longer really *ultimate*, there is no reason that it can't be "in" America and support American values. Competing with the mainstream churches, we find the religious theme parks where—for a price—one might even expect a miracle.

The veneer of religiosity that covers this form of atheism cannot conceal the fact that it has lost sight of the ultimate. For the religious atheist, the "devouring fire" of Deuteronomy chapter 4 verse 24 and the "hidden God" (*Deus absconditus*) portrayed in the writings of Martin Luther have lost all meaning; the ultimate has been tamed and reduced to categories that allow an easy integration into everyday life. One could call this a form of idolatry, but I prefer the phrase "religious atheism" for two reasons. First of all, idolatry in its historical forms possessed an element of seriousness that is lacking in contemporary religious atheism. The incantations of primitive religions may have grown out of a magical, mythological mode of thinking, but they were for the participants far more serious and closer to the ultimate than the glib slogans of the religious atheist. Secondly, the phrase "religious atheist" serves to highlight the similarities between this form and other forms of atheism. On an existential level, there is not a great deal of difference between ignoring the ultimate and trivializing the ultimate; in both cases, the ultimate ceases to be experienced as such.

The problem of religious atheism can be set in relief by considering the theological views of two well-known theologians: Martin Luther and Paul Tillich. In 1529, the German reformer Martin Luther composed the "Large Catechism" for instruction of the newly formed church communities of the Reformation. In his commentary on the First Commandment, "Thou shalt have no other gods before me", he writes:

> That is: You should consider me *alone* as your God. What is the force of this, and how is it to be understood? What does it mean to have a God? Or, what is God? Answer: A God means that from which we expect all good things and to which we take refuge in all distress. Thus to have a God is nothing else than to trust and believe Him from the heart; as I have often said that the trust and faith of the heart alone make both God and an idol. If your faith and trust be right, then is your God also true; and, on the other hand, if your trust be false and wrong, then you have not the true God; for these two belong together, faith and God. So I say: Upon which you set your heart and put your trust is properly your God. Therefore it is the intent of this commandment to require true faith and trust of the heart which settles upon the only true God and clings to him *alone*.[35]

It has often been noted that the First Commandment does not express a belief in monotheism, but rather calls the people of God to be faithful to one God alone. Luther interprets this aspect of the Commandment by introducing the correlation of God and faith and by emphasizing that faith always determines how God will be experienced. If a person believes that God is an angry, punishing God, then this person will experience God in this way. If, on the other hand, a person believes that God is merciful and loving, then he will experience God accordingly. Luther then proceeds to give a "definition" of God that allows for a variety of understandings: God is that from which we expect all good things and to which we take refuge in all distress. Based on this statement, "God" could take on a variety of forms: the material wealth of a person, the person's intellectual ability, the person's family and so forth. Whatever stabilizes the self of the person by promising good and by giving the assurance of safety in dire need, that becomes "God" for the person. There is much about Luther's view that still requires clarification, but for the moment, the most important aspect is the *exclusiveness* of the relationship between the person and God. If this God is really able to provide safety in all need, there can be only *one* true God, and this God must be ultimate in power and love. Then that which is less than ultimate cannot be trusted in the most severe crises of life.

Writing around the middle of the twentieth century, the Protestant theologian Paul Tillich provided an existential interpretation of Luther's commentary in the "Large Catechism" by coining the phrase "ultimate concern". The "ultimate" portion of the phrase refers to the unconditional, total and infinite character of the concern; the word "concern" points to the existential character of the experience. There are many preliminary concerns of great importance such as: art, music, poetry, natural science, political programs and social action. But a person can have only *one* ultimate, unconditional concern, and this concern becomes for him the existential center for organizing all other concerns. Tillich writes: "What *does* concern us unconditionally?...Nothing can be of ultimate concern for us which does not have the power of threatening and saving our being."[36(p14)] The word "being" means for Tillich "the whole of human reality, the structure, the meaning, and the aim of existence".[36(p14)] The ultimate concern of an individual is that which determines the whole of his reality. The ultimate concern determines the place of everything else in the person's life and experience. Just as Luther allowed for a variety of gods, from whom the person might expect all good things and help in times of need, so also Tillich recognized that individuals can choose from many different concerns the one that they consider "ultimate", but both theologians assumed that there is for each person only one "God" or one "ultimate concern" that provides unity to the self. It is, however, exactly this claim that seems to be untenable in our contemporary world.

Characteristic of our age is the complete loss of an *ultimate* concern. To be sure, we have a variety of relative concerns, one of them being religion, but none of these concerns is experienced as *ultimate*. This is the plight of the religious atheist. The obscuring of the bond between time and eternity has rendered all possible concerns as only relative. In the end, the religious atheist suffers from the same phenomenon of distraction and lack of focusing that is typical of the practical atheist. Only an ultimate concern can provide the centering necessary for the stability of the self, and in the absence of the ultimate, the self becomes diffused and unfocused, unable to pass sound judgment. Therefore, the religious atheist will in matters of ethics either appeal to the biblical tradition as an absolute rule of conduct or align himself with Enlightenment values by appealing to the concept of tolerance. In both cases, the religious atheist seeks an absolute standard outside of the self because the self lacks the necessary centering provided by the experience of the ultimate.

In this essay, I have dealt with three forms of atheism that can be observed in contemporary society, but it would be a mistake to view this analysis as comprehensive. Particularly with regard to the religious atheist, it should be emphasized that the category does not apply to every individual who professes a religious faith. Just as there are serious theoretical atheists who struggle with the most advanced forms of religion and come, nevertheless, to an atheistic conclusion, there are also serious believers in the religious community who are not guilty of trivializing the ultimate and who share much in common with the reformers of previous ages. Such exceptions, however, only confirm the analysis. We live in an age of distraction, which lends itself naturally to ignoring or trivializing the ultimate.

10

Beyond Atheism

"Does God exist?" Ask a Christian this question, and you will probably get as an answer a decisive "yes". Ask an atheist this question, and you will undoubtedly get an equally decisive "no". In the course of this talk, I will try to convince you that the Christian and the atheist have much more in common than they think. They are both treating the question "Does God exist?" as though it were a meaningful question that could be answered with a simple "yes" or "no". There are, however, several problems with the question, one being the word "exist". It would be interesting to analyze the question from this point of view, but the word "exist" would lead us too far into the area of existential philosophy. Therefore, I will comment only briefly on the word "exist" and concentrate my remarks on the other significant word in the question: "God". Furthermore, I will consider the word "God" from the standpoint of the Christian tradition for the simple reason that I understand this tradition better than I do others. I think a similar case could be made from the standpoint of the Jewish tradition since, as we know, Christianity was originally a sect of Judaism.

Let's start with the atheist, since dealing with the Christian's answer will be a bit more complicated. If the atheist seriously considers the question "Does God exist?", he must have some idea of what the word "God" means. After all, how could we say that something doesn't exist, if we don't know what is under consideration? If the word "God" has absolutely no meaning for the atheist, then the question itself is meaningless and consequently so is his answer to the question. Suppose that I ask the atheist this question: "Does the centrifugal bumble-puppy exist?" He may not feel comfortable answering with a simple "yes" or "no". He may well respond: "I don't know what 'centrifugal bumble-puppy' means, and therefore I can't say whether or not such a thing exists." But let's suppose that he is an atheist who has read Aldous Huxley's *Brave New World* and knows that a centrifugal bumble-puppy is not a thing, but rather a children's game. Then the atheist might well respond that the question makes no sense. How can you say that a game exists? Let's go a step further and suppose that six children are playing this game. Now if we ask the atheist his opinion about the existence of the six children, he will not hesitate to say that the children do, in fact, exist. But what if I ask him about the existence of the number six? Then, he may not so easily find an answer. Our entire world functions apparently on the basis of numbers. Can you imagine what would happen to our economy if all the numbers in the world suddenly disappeared? And yet, as important as numbers are, it is not clear that it makes any sense to say that they exist. Likewise, I want to say to our hypothetical atheist that it doesn't make any sense to ask the question: "Does God *exist*?" To this, he will undoubtedly object, saying to me that the word "God" refers to a being, and beings, unlike numbers, either exist or they don't exist. He may even go further and say: "Everybody knows what the word 'God' means; it refers to an all-powerful being, which is separate from the world but interacts causally with the world, and either this being exists or it doesn't exist." To which I will respond: "That's not, in my opinion, what the word 'God' means." And so here we are: Unless we agree on what the word "God" means, we can't answer the question: "Does God exist?"

The dilemma that we are facing has its origins in the seventeenth and eighteenth centuries. It is not unimportant to note that the term "atheist" is first attested in the latter part of the sixteenth century and did not come into frequent usage until the seventeenth century. Furthermore, we should note that the word is a privative like "atypical" or "asymmetrical". In 1678, the English philosopher Ralph Cudworth published his work *The True Intellectual System of the Universe*, in which he describes the atheist as one who is *not* a theist. The dichotomy between the theist and the atheist originated in the context of the developing scientific understandings of the seventeenth century, and this dichotomy dominated the religious discussion throughout the eighteenth century. To put it another way: We are dealing here with a problem that originated with the discoveries of men like Kepler, Galileo and Sir Isaac Newton. And it was precisely in relation to their discoveries that both the theists and the atheists defined the term "God".

The seventeenth century was in many ways a golden age in the intellectual tradition of England. At the beginning of the century, William Shakespeare was still living, and Francis Bacon was developing his views on scientific method. At the end of the century, there was John Milton and the philosopher John Locke. It was also the age of Thomas Hobbes, William Gilbert and William Harvey, but the undisputed genius in the area of natural science was Sir Isaac Newton. Alexander Pope wrote in a poem about Newton: "All Nature and its laws lay hid in Night. / God said, Let Newton be, and all was light." Newton was born in 1642, the same year that Galileo died, and he published his famous *Principia Mathematica* in 1687. What was groundbreaking about Newton's work was his insight into the laws of the entire known universe. Both Johannes Kepler and Galileo Galilei had made advances in the area of astronomy, and Galileo had also investigated the movement of bodies on the earth. But it was Newton who discovered that all material bodies, whether in the heavens or on the surface of the earth, obey the exact same laws. This breakthrough allowed a totally new understanding of the world, a unified understanding of the entire universe as one huge mechanism obeying the laws of cause and effect. Every event in the universe has a *cause*, and its cause can only be understood as a *force* or some combination of forces. A billiard ball moves toward the pocket on the billiard table because the cue ball has hit it, thus applying a force to it. The apple falls from the tree to the ground, because the gravitational force has acted on it. Every event is to be understood in terms of cause and effect, and the only admissible causes are forces that are measurable. For instance, the force applied to the billiard ball can be calculated as the product of the mass of the cue ball and its acceleration — the familiar $F = ma$.

The work of Newton was further developed by Leonard Euler and Joseph Louis Lagrange in the eighteenth century and led eventually to an understanding of what became known as the Newtonian World Machine, a closed nexus of cause and effect. In such a world, there is apparently no room for God to interact with human beings. Christian theologians and philosophers alike responded to this new worldview by redefining their understanding of God's action in the world. Admittedly, God cannot break the causal chain of the physical world, but in order to avoid an infinite regress in the chain, it seemed necessary to posit a *first* cause and this is, so it was maintained, what we mean when we say the word "God". God created the universe, set it in motion and then left it to operate on its own. Theologians and philosophers who maintained this view were called Deists (John Toland, Matthew Tindal, among others).

But not all Christian theologians were satisfied with this understanding of God, and here we arrive at the heart of our problematic. In contrast to the Deists, the so-called Theists wanted to maintain that God could also interact with human beings in the world by *interrupting* the causal chain and producing His own effects. The Theists conceived of God not only as the *creator* of the world, but also as an *agent* in the world. According to them, God is a being separate from the world, that is characterized by goodness and that can act in the world to bring about this or that change. Since the Newtonian World Machine is a huge nexus of cause and effect, the action of God in the world must also be postulated in terms of cause and effect. God's action is the cause; the change in the world is the effect. Once the word "God" is defined in these terms, all sorts of problems arise. If God can interrupt the causal chain and produce this or that effect in the world, why doesn't He prevent natural catastrophes, why doesn't He cure illnesses, why did He allow the Holocaust to happen, and the list goes on. Given this context, the atheists of the period had the more convincing argument. They held that such a being, that is, a being that is good and that is able to cause things to happen in the world, could not possibly exist. The playwright Archibald MacLeish gave expression to this view in his classic play *JB*: "If God is God He is not good. If God is good He is not God." The atheist argues that the notion of a being that is both good and able to causally alter the course of events in the world is logically inconsistent with the undeniable fact of misfortune and suffering in the world. Therefore, God does not exist. Try as he may, the theist has difficulty answering the objection of the atheist. He might try to explain suffering and misfortune as a punishment for sin or as a type of divine instruction, but in the end, it is hardly plausible to interpret a catastrophe such as Hurricane Katrina in this way. What were the dead supposed to learn? And what was the sin of the newborn baby?

Our primary interest today is not, however, to find an answer to the problem of human suffering, but rather to move beyond the dichotomy of theism and atheism. The atheist fails to realize that his denial of God is based on a particular understanding of God—an understanding that is rooted in Newtonian physics. The theist, for his part, fails to realize that his understanding of God is not only untenable; it does not correspond to any historical religion, certainly not to the Christian tradition. In order to move beyond the dichotomy of theism and atheism, we must find a point of departure for our thinking that focuses on the elementary experiences of human existence. One possibility would be to consider the parables of Jesus as they are recorded in the New Testament since parables as such are expressive of existential concerns.

If we put aside the dogma of the Christian Church, if we bracket out the myth of creation and the legendary elements of the miracles, and if we simply read the parables of Jesus, we are struck at once by their everydayness. It is indeed striking how seldom Jesus uses the word "God". He talks about a sower going out to sow seed. He talks about a good Samaritan, about a treasure in a field, about a great banquet, about a prodigal son, about an unforgiving servant. But surprising as it may seem, Jesus does not have much to say directly about God. He talks about everyday people in everyday situations, and yet the way in which he talks about these things allows us to see them in a new light. Consider, for example, the parable of the "Good Samaritan". In the first-century Jewish community, the phrase "Love your neighbor as yourself" was much debated, and on one occasion, the question was put to Jesus: "Who is my neighbor?" In reply he related this parable:

A man was going down from Jerusalem to Jericho, when he was attacked by robbers. They stripped him of his clothes, beat him and went away, leaving him half dead. A priest happened to be going down the same road, and when he saw the man, he passed by on the other side. So too, a Levite, when he came to the place and saw him, passed by on the other side. But a Samaritan, as he traveled, came where the man was; and when he saw him, he took pity on him. He went to him and bandaged his wounds, pouring on oil and wine. Then he put the man on his own donkey, brought him to an inn and took care of him. The next day he took out two denarii and gave them to the innkeeper. "Look after him," he said, "and when I return, I will reimburse you for any extra expense you may have." (Then Jesus asked:) "Which of these three do you think was a neighbor to the man who fell into the hands of robbers?" The man who had placed the question about the neighbor replied, "The one who had mercy on him." Jesus told him, "Go and do likewise."

This parable, which is recorded in the Gospel of Luke chapter 10, is so well known that we often fail to recognize its uniqueness. Without going into detail, there are three elements that require our attention. As we noted, the parable is presented as an answer to the question: "Who is my neighbor?" This question was vigorously debated in the first century and is still relevant today. It has to do with the *limits* of moral obligation. If it is true that assisting our neighbor is a moral obligation, who counts as our neighbor: relatives, people in our neighborhood, individuals with whom we share a common interest (in a club), members of our religious affiliation, Americans or in general English-speaking peoples? Where are the limits of moral obligation?

The first point to note about the parable is that it simply does not answer this question. Instead of defining the limits of moral obligation, it paints for us a picture of a situation in which the person acting is neighborly. The neighbor is not the person who *needed* help, but rather the person who *provided* help. In essence, the parable refuses to set any limits to moral obligation and shows us a world in which the question has no meaning. The second point is this: To our great surprise the neighbor in this parable is not the priest, but rather the half-breed Samaritan. The Samaritans were not particularly well liked and certainly not respected in the same way as the priests were. So measured on the standards of that day, the parable does not have a very satisfying ending. Now here is the third and crucial point. By refusing to set limits on moral obligation and by inverting the roles of the priest and the Samaritan, the parable turns an everyday situation upside down. Our everyday world looks suddenly strange. It is our world, and yet not our world. It is familiar, and yet unfamiliar. It is as though we had stepped through Alice's looking glass. Things are oddly familiar and yet no longer in their proper place. And it is precisely this familiar/unfamiliar world that becomes our point of departure for thinking about God. For the message of Jesus on this point is clear: When the divine presence draws near, our world is transformed so that the familiar becomes strangely unfamiliar. The *everydayness* is disclosed in its *uniqueness*.

I want now to leave the Christian tradition and take up an everyday situation with which all of us are familiar: our involvement in the process of self-actualization. The term "self-actualization" has been used in various theories of psychology, but for the moment, it suffices to understand the term as Carl Rogers did, that is, as a human being's actualizing of his potentialities. Carl Rogers understood the process of self-actualization as an alternative to the depth psychology of Freud as well as to the behaviorism of B. F. Skinner. According to Rogers, the self is similar to an organism with innate potentialities that can be developed and actualized. Such self-actualization takes place through formal education, through individual training (such as, when one develops a musical talent) or through participation in various sorts of encounter groups. The success of such groups is, in my opinion, indisputable. And equally indisputable is the desire of human beings to develop themselves as much as possible. From the cradle to the grave, we spend an enormous amount of time and expend an enormous amount of energy trying to develop ourselves. The reference to the time span from the cradle to the grave introduces, however, an apparently insurmountable problem. All of our efforts to develop and actualize ourselves occur on a finite timeline whose terminal point we can already anticipate. Life appears as a one-way street, and regardless of how much we develop ourselves, the street always leads to a dead end where everything that we have accomplished is destroyed.

Around the middle of the nineteenth century, there lived in Concord, Massachusetts, three authors: Ralph Waldo Emerson, Henry David Thoreau and Nathaniel Hawthorne. In one of his essays, entitled "The Old Manse" (1846), Hawthorne wrote about the inexorable movement from life to death:

> How early in the summer, too, the prophecy of autumn comes! Earlier in some years than in others; sometimes even in the first weeks of July. There is no other feeling like what is caused by this faint, doubtful, yet real perception—if it be not rather a foreboding—of the year's decay, so blessedly sweet and sad in the same breath. Did I say that there was no feeling like it? Ah, but there is a half-acknowledged melancholy like to this when we stand in the perfected vigor of our life and feel that Time has now given us all his flowers, and that the next work of his never idle fingers must be to steal them one by one away.[37(p67f)]

We develop ourselves, we attain a level of education, we pursue the arts, we strive toward perfection, and when we stand in the perfected vigor of life, we sense that time is about to take away everything that we have attained. Step by step our lives are diminished, and we are visited by a spirit of melancholy that no self-actualization can remove. Time shows us its character as the unavoidable slope from life to death, and we realize that the experience of loss is fundamental to human existence.

But if we reflect back on our lives, we will realize that the experience of loss does not only occur as we grow older. The experience of loss is fundamental to the movement of time itself. As children, we lost the immediacy of our environment when we learned language. It is the acquisition of language that allows us to transcend the immediacy of the moment, to think back on the past and to plan the future. As adults, we have lost the innocence of childhood. Perhaps we married and had children. How adorable the children were! And we probably took pictures of our children. Did you ever ask yourself why you took those pictures? Was it not to preserve the immediacy of the moment? Did you not realize, even if only vaguely, that the moment was passing away and would be lost forever if you didn't capture it in a picture? And yet the picture is not the real thing. The moment does pass, the immediacy is lost, and time moves on.

This is not, however, our only experience of time. There are elevated moments of life, moments of intense joy, in which we experience a *completion* of time, a *fullness* of time, whereby past and future seem to coalesce in the present. This experience of the fullness of time without a hint of loss, untainted by melancholy, is the experience of *eternity* in time. Plato described time as the moving image of eternity. In order to understand this statement, we must first distinguish between eternal and everlasting. Everlasting indicates a temporal continuation without end. If we could live forever, we would be everlasting, but not eternal. The eternal is interwoven with the moment; it is a particular way in which time occurs. Eternity is the experience of the fullness of time, the experience of life as complete. When the eternal manifests itself in time, we experience life as it should be. Everything is in its place. Nothing is missing; nothing is lost.

Admittedly, there are few such moments in life, but it is precisely these moments that provide to us a point of departure for thinking about God. Earlier, I talked about the parable of the "Good Samaritan". This parable is not simply a moral lesson; it shows us how human relationships are experienced when the divine presence draws near. Likewise, the manifestation of the eternal in time shows us the experience of time in the presence of the divine. Eternal life is not everlasting life; it is the manifestation of the eternal in time, the experience of the fullness of life. From this perspective, the question: "Does God exist?" becomes oddly irrelevant. What we need in our daily lives is not a theory about the existence of a being separate from the universe that interacts causally with the universe, about how such a being could have created the universe and so forth. All such discussions remain paradoxically on the plane of scientific thinking and do little to enhance our lives. What we need in our daily lives is a new way of experiencing relationships and a new way of experiencing the movement of time, in short, an *existential transformation* that in religious language is called eternal life. It is my conviction that we can move beyond atheism to a viable understanding of religion that is enriching, not restricting, that is existential, not theoretical—an understanding of religion that is in the best sense humanistic, not humanistic in the sense that it rejects the reality of God and limits itself to an empirical view of human nature, but rather humanistic in the sense that it enriches the human condition, that it allows human beings to be the very best that they can be, by opening up access to the divine presence through elementary experiences such as that between time and eternity. Moving beyond atheism in this way may or may not be welcomed by contemporary religious leaders. That is, however, of secondary importance. The value in moving beyond atheism is not to rescue some failing institution of religion, but rather to enrich the lives of human beings.

References

1   Augustine. Confessions. Book 11, Chapter 17.

2   Plato. Timaios. 37d5.

3   Becker G. The Economic Approach to Human Behavior. Chicago: The University of Chicago Press; 1976.

4   Stearns PN. Consumerism in World History: The Global Transformation of Desire. 2nd ed. New York: Routledge; 2006.

5   Berner A, Tonder CL van. The Postmodern Consumer: Implications of Changing Customer Expectations for Organisation Development in Service Organisations. SA Journal of Industrial Psychology. 2003; 29(3):7–10.

6   Koppelman A. Judging the Case against Same-Sex Marriage. University of Illinois Law Review. 2014 May; (2):431–465.

7   Finnis J. Human Rights and the Common Good. Collected Essays: Volume 3. Oxford: Oxford University Press; 2011. Part 6.

8   Koppelman A. Three arguments for gay rights. The Michigan Law Review. 1997 May; 95(6)1636–1667.

9   Ettelbrick P. Since When Is Marriage a Path to Liberation? Out/Look: National Lesbian and Gay Quarterly. 1989 Fall; 14–17.

10   Ettelbrick P, Shapiro J. Are We on the Path to Liberation Now? Same-Sex Marriage at Home and Abroad. Seattle Journal for Social Justice. 2004; 2(2):475–493.

11   Rotello G. Creating a New Gay Culture: Balancing Fidelity and Freedom. The Nation. 1997 April 21; 11–16.

12   Firestone R. Holy War in Modern Judaism? "Mitzvah War" and the Problem of the "Three Vows". Journal of the American Academy of Religion. 2006; 74(4):954–982.

13   Liebs D. Bellum iustum in Theorie und Praxis. In: Martin Avenarius (ed.). Ars iuris: Festschrift für Okko Behrends

zum 70. Geburtstag. Göttingen: Wallstein; 2009. p. 305–318.

14 Kelly C. The End of Empire: Attila the Hun and the Fall of Rome. New York: W. W. Norton; 2009.

15 Fordyce J. Aspects of Scepticism. London: Elliot Stock; 1883.

16 Paley W. Natural Theology or Evidence of the Existence and Attributes of the Deity, collected from the appearances of nature (1802). Oxford: Oxford University Press; 2008.

17 Darwin C. The Descent of Man. vol. 1. London: John Murray; 1871.

18 Carnegie A. Wealth. The North American Review. 1889; 148(391):653–665.

19 Prasad A. Virgin conception would be more plausible if Mary was a man. 2008 Dec. Available from: http://www.the guardian.com/science/blog/2008/dec/30/virgin-birth-mary.

20 Brunner-Traut E. Die Geburtsgeschichte der Evangelien im Lichte ägyptologischer Forschungen. Zeitschrift für Religions- und Geistesgeschichte. 1960; 12(2):97–111.

21 Kafka F. Parables and Paradoxes. New York: Schocken Books; 1961.

22 Jammer M. Concepts of Force. (1957) Mineola, New York: Dover Publications, Inc.; 1999.

23 Newton I. Opticks. Query 31 (2nd ed. 1717). Opera, vol. 4; 1988.

24 Einstein A. Ideas and Opinions. New York: Bonanza Books; 1954.

25 Capra F. The Tao of Physics. Berkeley: Random House; 1975.

26 Locke J. Two Treatises of Government (1690). ed. Peter Laslett. Cambridge: Cambridge University Press; 1988.

27 Cicero. On the Laws. In: On the Commonwealth and On the Laws. ed. James Zetzel. Cambridge: Cambridge University Press; 1999. p. 105–175.

28 Cicero. On the Commonwealth. In: On the Commonwealth and On the Laws. ed. James Zetzel. Cambridge: Cambridge University Press; 1999. p. 1–103.

29 Hobbes T. Leviathan. Cambridge: Cambridge University Press; 1996.

30 Spencer H. The Man versus the State. Caldwell, Idaho: The Caxton Printers Ltd.; 1960.

31 Plato. The Republic. Book 4. 433a.

32 Cicero. On Duties. Cambridge: Cambridge University Press; 1991.

33 Tillich P. The Idea of the Personal God. The Union Review. 1940 Nov; 2(1):8–10.

34 Arendt H. Society and Culture. Daedalus. 1960; 89(2):278–287.

35 Luther M. The Large Catechism. In: The Book of Concord: The Confessions of the Evangelical Lutheran Church. Philadelphia: Fortress Press; 1959.

36 Tillich P. Systematic Theology. Three volumes in one. Chicago: The University of Chicago Press; 1967.

37 Hawthorne N. The Old Manse. Sandwich, MA: Chapman Billies; 1997.

BOOKS

Iff Books is interested in ideas and reasoning. It publishes material on science, philosophy and law. Iff Books aims to work with authors and titles that augment our understanding of the human condition, society and civilisation, and the world or universe in which we live.